IRRESPONSIBLY
DIGITAL

HOW TO SURVIVE MARKETING'S
EXISTENTIAL CRISIS

Abe Kasbo

Design and typesetting by Diana Ghazzawi/Wordreams
Cartoons by Tom Fishburne, the Marketoonist

Paperback ISBN: 979-8-9991614-0-6
ebook ISBN: 979-8-9991614-1-3

Contents

Acknowledgments

To Anna: Thank you for your unwavering support, endless patience, and the countless hours you spent listening to my ideas, calming my doubts, and cheering me on. This book, and everything else I do, would not exist without your love, encouragement, and willingness to shoulder extra responsibilities so I could pursue my work. You are my greatest blessing.

To my team at Verasoni and our amazing clients, thank you for being an abundant source of inspiration for every idea and word in this book.

Peppered throughout this book are cartoons from Tom Fishburne, the Marketoonist. Tom's cartoons use humor and levity to help explain the reality of our marketing world like no other. He began creating cartoons during his time at Harvard Business School, initially sharing them with colleagues in 2002. Since then, Tom's good humor and critique of marketing have gained widespread popularity in the business world. I hope they make for fun companions along your read.

Introduction

Let's be clear: the world doesn't need another marketing book. Not when an online search for "marketing" floods your screen with 100,000 hollow promises. But this? This isn't a book. It's a code red for the soul of marketing, a discipline hijacked by the very tools it needs.

Marketing indeed is going through a crisis. Others will surely pour cold water over my assertion and say that's just the natural progression of business responding to technology and our economic zeitgeist. And while that may be true, it's not remotely the most interesting part of the story. Marketers live inside a paradox, a world where humanity's greatest connective leaps—social media, smartphones, instant global intimacy—have turned us into data livestock, economic units. Every click, swipe, and tap fatten algorithms that gorge on and stalk us, not to serve, but to seduce, manipulate, and sometimes ensure compliance. In the wake of all of these technological leaps, many disciplines, including marketing, have been laid to waste. In the coming pages, you'll find marketing's challenges illustrated with a combination of data, real life examples, and humor. Some of this may feel uncomfortable. Please fade your feelings and, as the kids say these days, buckle up!

People rage against ads yet crave the dopamine drip of novelty: the green lime squeezer, which is a lemon squeezer, but you'll buy one because it's green and another because it's yellow. Why? Because that's what we marketers tell people to do. Our job is to entice, tempt, and convince people to buy our stuff. Worse, we as consumers, egged on by marketers, are hostages of mindshare, our wallets held ransom by brands that hack our attention spans, but not necessarily earn our loyalty.

This book is about what marketing has become: a short-term casino where CMOs bet on vanity metrics, chasing viral jackpots while their brands rot from within. The rise of "digital first" dogma has gutted strategy, replacing it with a desperate scramble for likes, a race where even "winning" could mean losing. For example, studies now reveal what instinct already screams: organic reach on platforms is a myth, a rigged game where brands pay to shout into hurricanes. Yet marketers keep shooting up on digital meth, addicted to the illusion of control, pacified by daily doses of analytics dopamine.

This book is not nostalgia. Its primary function is to help the reader understand the marketing landscape, opportunities, and pitfalls, and maximize value from the marketing enterprise. No, it's not a plea to resurrect Mad Men–era billboards or spam your inbox with "thought leadership" and white papers. It's a call to arms for marketers and businesses who've forgotten they're meant to build, not beg. To create value, not vomit content. To treat audiences as partners, not prey.

The rot runs deep. Boardrooms now reduce marketing to "KPI management," as if brands are Excel cells to be filled, not legacies to be nurtured. We've bred a generation of marketers fluent in click-through rates but illiterate in culture, trading creativity for clickbait.

But here's the secret they'll hate me for saying: the addiction ends here. Reclaiming marketing doesn't mean abandoning digital; it means dominating it, not as slaves to feeds, but as architects of meaning. It means ruthless ROI on humanity, not just revenue.

The future belongs to those brave enough to ask, "What if we marketed more intently...and mattered more?" This book is your defibrillator. Use it before your business flatlines. As you read, take time to put it down and think about the concepts I'm sharing. Check my math if you need to feel better. The material here challenges the prevailing world view, and it will challenge yours. There's a lot in here to make readers uncomfortable, and I am good with that.

> **"Do what you do so well that they will want to see it again and bring their friends."**
>
> —Walt Disney

In many ways, none of the ideas and concepts that this book offers are new; they've simply been drowned out for about 20 years by typhoons of digital nonsense. I'm not just talking to marketers in this book. While the principles in these pages will undeniably be useful to marketing pros, I am writing for CEOs, CFOs, board members, and the associate assistant account executive in companies of all sizes who need a sober and fresh perspective on the "now, everything, all at once" approach to marketing that seems to have engulfed our zeitgeist. I'll get right to the point here: marketing as a profession needs to recover from its relatively recent addiction and abuses of all things digital and the hegemony of AdTech. Just as with any recovery, we must first recognize the illness or the addiction, the damage it's causing, and get to the root of the problem. The time for bold action is now. This book throws sunshine where there's none, shade on marketing shenanigans, and makes the case for sober marketing strategies, context, and pathways. It is my hope the words on these pages give you, the reader, more clarity in an increasingly murky, hamster-wheel marketing space, to help you make better, smarter marketing decisions, whatever business or sector you're in.

The Birth of Marketing Madness: I Was There

I started Verasoni in 2005 when our twins were 3 months old. At the time, Amazon was 11 years old, Google was 7, and Facebook was a gleam in Zuckerberg's eyes and would be born about a year later, in 2006. From the start, as both a participant and a student of the marketing game, I got to see and experience digital marketing's almost immediate chokehold on everything else marketing with shocking precision. Not only did digital marketing suck budgets from other marketing channels, but it also simultaneously created doubt in what we now call legacy channels and platforms in the minds of many marketers and business leaders, which automatically eliminated them from consideration as viable marketing strategies. So, Verasoni was born under these conditions and currently thrives in this dynamic.

We've seen this story before, the manic drumbeat of "next big things" pounding boardroom tables into splinters. First, it was SEO, QR codes, and the relentless chant of "Post to Facebook!" Now, the fever dream repeats: ChatGPT, TikTok, and the desperate scramble to plant flags on algorithmic quicksand. Clients, wide-eyed and ravenous, demand miracles from platforms still learning to crawl, while dismissing legacy strategies as relics. But here's the brutal truth: digital marketing's greatest trick isn't innovation; it's convincing us every shiny toy will rewrite the rules of gravity. I'm sure as you're reading these words, you're feeling AI, right?

Across industries, healthcare, retail, even farming, the same delusion persists. Hospital CEOs lament that their LinkedIn posts don't viralize like a coffee shop's latte art. Family-owned farms fret over TikTok follower counts as if they're competing with Nike. The refrain echoes, "If they're doing it, why can't we?" As if industries with diametric purposes could harvest the same soil. This isn't strategy; it's collective psychosis, a cargo cult of metrics divorced from meaning.

Digital platforms mutate faster than viruses. What worked six months ago is obsolete today. Yet, the hunger for overnight empire-building remains unchanged, a relic of the early 2000s, when MySpace still felt revolutionary. We've conflated presence with power, posting for relevance, mistaking the map for the territory. But let's autopsy the carnage. Digital didn't just disrupt; it bombed everything in its way into oblivion. Television, newspapers, radio? Reduced to relative rubble, their once-monolithic influence scattered to the winds. In their place, tech bros and influencers rise like phoenixes, while politicians and governments weaponize feeds to sculpt ideologies. The stakes? Control over how ideas are bought, sold, and believed.

Yet, for all its pyrotechnics, digital's victory is incomplete. Legacy media lingers, not as a corpse, but a ghost. Newspapers still sway elections. TV ads still move millions. But to admit this is heresy in an age addicted to the dopamine of "disruption."

In our race to deify digital, we've ignored its darkest trade-off. Yes, it democratizes fame and connects continents, but it also reduces culture to clickbait, brands to bots, and vital business strategy to a slot machine. We've traded the cathedral of storytelling for the carnival of virality.

The question isn't "How do we keep up?" It's "Why are we still playing a rigged game?" Despite the supposed evidence and momentum, the future belongs not to those chasing algorithms, but to those rewriting them, or walking away entirely. Legacy media's coffin remains open. Will you nail it shut, or dare to resurrect its bones? Many marketing leaders are aware of the issues I raise in this book, but they either ignore them or slow walk their business for reasons I delve into later in these pages, including self-preservation.

The breakneck evolution of digital tools, from AI to viral platforms, has turned marketing into a battlefield where hype often overshadows substance. Yet, amid the chaos and fog of war, the core principles of marketing remain unshaken: seize attention, forge connection, and drive action. These timeless truths cut through the noise, whether you're Coca-Cola, whose Share a Coke campaign fused AI-driven personalization with the universal craving for belonging, or Hims, which shattered taboos with bold, attention-grabbing ads before building trust through sleek, relatable branding. Technology is a tool, not a strategy. Every trend must be stress-tested against marketing's fundamentals: Does it command attention? Does it spark emotion? Does it compel action?

Marketing's power lies in its diverse arsenal of disciplines, each a precision instrument for specific challenges. Advertising isn't just about selling products; it's about owning cultural real estate, like Home Depot's mastery of the "home improvement" mindset. Influencers wield modern-day word-of-mouth, as seen when a single TikTok video propelled Prime Energy Drink into a $250 million phenomenon. Public relations is narrative warfare: Target's decision to double down on LGBTQ+ partnerships during backlash wasn't just damage control; it was a defiant reinforcement of brand identity. And events? Apple's product launches aren't mere announcements; they're cultural earthquakes, like the 2007 iPhone debut that redefined communication. The key is to choose your weapons wisely, blending disciplines to attack problems from all angles.

AI amplifies both opportunity and risk. A generic, algorithm-generated ad might chase clicks, regardless of whether they're human or not, but erode brand soul, like the forgettable YouTube pre-roll ads we instinctively skip. True power emerges when human intuition partners with machines. To master this balance, marketers must learn to audit hype ruthlessly, which is not an easy task, nor is it in our cultural DNA. Netflix uses AI to recommend content, but greenlit *Stranger Things* because creators pitched a vibe, nostalgia, mystery, and rebellion that data alone couldn't quantify. Walmart's revival of "everyday low prices" paired AI-driven inventory systems with human-crafted ads that resonated with real-life struggles. Nike's Dream Crazy campaign, starring Colin Kaepernick, defied data-driven caution to electrify its audience, winning an Emmy and boosting sales. Data informs, but instinct inspires.

Survival in this arena demands owning a category so fiercely that your brand becomes synonymous with an idea and feelings about that idea. Red Bull equals extreme sports. Tesla equals electric revolution. Lume carved a niche with "whole body deodorant," transforming a commodity into a mission. For marketers, the ultimate test is synthesis: Imagine launching a sustainable sneaker brand. How would you hijack attention and keep it beyond the scroll? A TikTok stunt with influencers scaling skyscrapers in your shoes? What story would hook hearts: highlighting recycled materials or partnering with Greta Thunberg or Al Gore to embody eco-activism? Or would that represent a risk to your brand? What "buy now" trigger would you pull: scarcity, social proof, or a viral challenge? The answer lies in weaponizing brand principles first, not fleeting trends.

The future of marketing isn't about outsmarting algorithms; it's about out-feeling them. Marketing technology can optimize, but it can't replicate the human truths of desire, fear, or belonging (for the foreseeable future). Those who thrive will fuse technology with timeless intuition, turning hype into horsepower and chaos into legacy. The question isn't what tools you'll use, but what story you'll tell, and whether it's bold enough to echo beyond the noise.

Like most people reading here, I grew up in a world bombarded by marketing. My interest in marketing started as a child in Aleppo, Syria, in the 1970s. I recall a steamy July afternoon in 1977. My father and I were sipping a Pepsi in his air condition–less box of a tailor shop, both dripping with sweat. Pepsi was a special treat we looked forward to about once a week. Back then, Pepsi didn't join us for dinner every night like it does in many homes around the world now. Soft drinks like Pepsi, 7Up, and Crush were considered delightful treats we looked forward to and enjoyed occasionally. On a hot July afternoon in July of 1977, as my father was checking his yarn and fabric inventory, I sat at his desk, reading a Donald Duck comic book (yes, we had those in Syria, and in Arabic to boot). I blurted something like, "Why are American products so much fun?" I quickly pointed to my book and held up the Pepsi can like the Statue of Liberty holding her torch, "How do these things end up in Aleppo all the way from America, and why do we buy them?" Seven-year-old me wasn't so much asking for an international trade thesis as much as I was trying to figure out how Pepsi and Donald Duck ended up in my boyish hands and how I came to know about them in the first place. And why these specific products? What makes people like them and buy them? Why am I reading a Disney book and drinking brown sugar water from a can with the colors of the American flag? And perhaps the most important question I asked frequently of myself and the adults around me was "Why do people talk about America so much?"

It was only after we immigrated to the United States in 1980 that I realized while living in Aleppo, I was reading, watching, touching, living, and even breathing (through secondhand smoke, usually Marlboro) the most powerful, addictive brand on Earth: the United States of America. In the 1970s, Buicks and Cadillacs, some from the 1950s, patrolled Qostaki Homsi Boulevard in Aleppo's fashionable Azzizieh neighborhood where I grew up. My eyes feasted on American automotive ingenuity, and I fell for young Laura Ingalls (played by Melissa Gilbert) on *Little House on the Prairie*. When I paged through Disney or DC Comics, I was transported to an otherworldly dimension where Superman and Batman always won their battles, Pa Ingalls always came through, and the Six Million Dollar Man always prevailed; all of these seemed to be grounded in American culture and values.

Every brand—Buick, Disney, Superman, Batman—was built on the omnipresent platform of the American brand. So, we couldn't see a Cadillac, smoke Marlboro, slip into Lee Jeans, or catch an episode of Woody Woodpecker without at least thinking of or feeling America's influence, or "Amayrka," as we called it. And there was a special bonus! You mean you can get all this cool stuff plus freedom of expression and you get to vote in a democracy where your vote matters? You mean you don't have to worry about what you say about your government? No wonder why everyone wanted to go to America! If American storytelling and products are so good in Aleppo, can you imagine what life could be like in New York, Chicago, or Thousand Oaks, California? *Yalla*, sign me up! *Yalla* means "let's go" in Arabic, so yeah, *yalla*!

I don't have a formal degree in business or marketing but learned in my early twenties I enjoyed connecting people to ideas, and marketing communications seemed a great way to do that. I was and continue to be fascinated in particular by how people, organizations, and even political movements, religions, and countries use language, images, and symbolism through storytelling to influence people or change their behavior. Much of what I've learned over my career has been by observing and doing.

There's one more thing that prepared me for the marketing game. I'm a long-time hoops coach and now serve as head girls varsity basketball coach at a school in North Jersey. I also served as Head Men's Basketball Coach at Centenary College (now University) in Hackettstown, New Jersey. I've always thought of coaching as a profession or avocation for entrepreneurs and marketers. Successful coaches are great teachers and better communicators and marketers. Today, I apply a coaching mindset to my marketing work. I sold players on everything from coming to practice on time, focusing on academics, becoming less selfish, playing more defense, having more confidence...you name it. Each team was my customer, each player a customer segment. When something didn't work in a game, we adjusted. And while I always take losses personally, I welcomed the opportunity, however painful or uncomfortable, to learn and adjust for the next game. And just as seasoned coaches fully recognize that winning a game isn't a given, but every game must be played, experienced marketers know not every campaign will be successful, but it must be competitive.

Finally, great coaches and marketers keep learning, adapting, and reflecting because the market, much like a basketball and everything else in life, is dynamic. Success or failure sometimes can depend on the competition or timing, sometimes squarely on campaign design and execution, and sometimes on dumb luck. Yes, luck. Yeah, they don't teach us that in school either. Just as players and coaches should neither fall in love with or dwell on game statistics, nor get bogged down by bad performances, marketers should not revel nor worry about their momentary analytics. When you buy the hype for any given game, you're finished in basketball and business. Be on the lookout for basketball references peppered here because competition is the corner where basketball and business meet in my mind.

> "Whatever coaching and leadership skills I possess were learned through listening, observation, study, and then trial and error along the way."
>
> —John Wooden

It is my hope this book makes the undiscussable discussable by separating hype from reality to establish a baseline for sensible marketing strategy. There's a lot to unpack and even more to unlearn.

1

Hail to the Clickocracy

To compete and win in basketball or other sports, you need good players who know how to play. Everyone can say they're a player, but not everyone can play. People who play basketball are not necessarily basketball players. Anyone can say they can shoot hoops, and in their eyes, they may think they shoot like Steph Curry, but the reality is they can't. Basketball is beloved around the world because anyone can play it, but not everyone can play well, let alone at the highest levels. Only a select few can do that. You see Steph's shot is the result of many things that people either don't see or understand. Of course, it's about practice and repetition. But it's also a result of his basketball IQ, his positioning of where and how he catches the ball in different areas of the court and at different times. His incredible shot is *the end result* of that hard work *combined* with countless other things, like running his man off several picks or not taking the pick at all. How Steph repositions himself after passing to a teammate and a plethora of in-the-moment decisions based on his calculus of the situation. Basketball IQ underlies Steph's incredibly reliable shooting. But what gets us off our seats is the shot. The same applies for marketing or any other field. Marketing IQ is critical to any marketing success. It's underlying work, understanding of the game, that make marketers great. Like basketball, not all marketers have the talent nor willingness to put in the work, to be great. So yeah, marketing IQ matters.

Before you throw this book in the trash and accuse me of being an elitist, step back and think about what I'm saying. Hear me out. It doesn't matter that people have an MBA in marketing from a brand name university and they've been in the field for ten years and so on. It means they received a degree; it doesn't mean they know what they're doing, no matter how long they've been doing it. So many people in marketing fake it till they make it in marketing, and that's cool, if they make it. Others fake it all the way till retirement or a buy-out. In marketing, it's easier than ever to fake it. But I imagine every field is afflicted with this condition.

Since 2005, people have poured into marketing because the field was busted wide open by the new digital possibilities making it "easier" than ever to be "in marketing." So as digital and social media have become more important to businesses, marketing was becoming swiftly democratized, and naturally the number of marketing positions have increased accordingly. Yet marketing, led by the irresistible lure of digital, has been subjected to the same reductive thinking that ESPN has brought to basketball, which continues on social media. Most basketball observers would agree that ESPN's approach to programming and use of highlights has effectively reduced basketball to three-pointers and crazy dunks. All of this happened well before digital took hold in 2005. Soundbite basketball—and all sports for that matter—on ESPN reduced the attention span of players and fans to the detriment of the game. The game, of course, is much more nuanced than breathtaking threes and thunderous dunks. The same parallel can be made in marketing; going viral is what people talk about, along with latching on to a trending hashtag. Of course, those can be important, but they are not the game. I'm fairly certain that I have just as good of a shot at making an NBA team as I do creating a viral campaign. I'm also fairly certain that some reader is reading this and muttering, "That's because *you* don't know what you're doing! LOL!" You see, not all marketing talent is equal. I am a guard and so is Michael Jordan. Who would you like playing for your team, me or Jordan?

Democratized marketing is a good thing. It opened doors that were previously closed to most people and brands. But it also happens to be a breeding ground for marketing mediocrity, leaving seasoned marketers, CEOs, and business owners bewildered and frustrated at times. While marketing pros rarely openly admit to the fog of marketing, they certainly complain about it in private. As I write, marketing continues its frantic march to gamification, chasing eyeballs, clicks, and attention spans, led loudly and proudly by what I call "Clickocrats." Clickocrats patrol the digital marketing echo chamber with the self-confidence and shallowness of Caillou. Clickocrats are digital marketing enthusiasts who often scoff at nondigital marketing strategies, however valid and reliable. They see nondigital marketing as a nonstarter or unimaginative, and seemingly have no time or patience for integrated campaigns because they're addicted to the hits of clicks, even if those clicks are not generated by humans—we'll get to that later.

Before we go any further, let's examine how to identify Clickocrats. These people are everywhere and can easily be spotted. You can identify them by listening carefully. They usually say stuff like the following:

- "Website visits are down/up."
- "Let me pull up the analytics."
- "Content is king."
- "We need a podcast."
- "How many clicks have we gotten on our site this week?"
- "We're working on a digital campaign and looking for it to go viral."
- "We'll just do Google Ads."
- "Our hashtag research shows that we can trend."
- "We're launching with a PPC campaign and homepage takeovers."
- "We're mapping the digital customer journey."

The Gospel According to Clickocrats (Blessed Be Their Algorithms)

These digital evangelists preach that success hangs on two holy relics: a viral post and a spreadsheet. Data, they chant, is the sacred scripture. Never mind that most business decisions, like, say, not setting your budget on fire, require less "analytics" and more common sense. But sure, Elon Musk built SpaceX because he A/B tested rocket emojis on Twitter. His real secret? Knowing people who can fund rockets, electric car factories, and social media platforms. Data, schmata. The Clickocrat's playbook? Often sleight-of-hand. They'll dazzle you with dashboards and click-through rates (CTRs), only to mask their creative bankruptcy and strategic illiteracy. "Look at the metrics!" they cry, as if clicks or likes pay the bills. Their true genius? Convincing CEOs that digital marketing is "cheaper" (spoiler: it's not), "trackable" (to the last penny wasted), and "easy" (if you ignore the 47 platforms, 12 agencies, and 3 existential crises required to run it).

> **"There are more fake guides, teachers in the world than stars. The real guide is the one who makes you see your inner beauty, not the one who wants to be admired and followed."**
>
> — Shams Tabrizi

Why bother with pesky things like psychology or storytelling when you can just "create content" and "post to social media"? Who needs to consider product lifecycles, price, demand, and timing when you've got social media trends? Clickocrats don't sell strategy; they sell compliance—a devoted compliance that funnels your dollars straight into the gaping maw of AdTech firms, "digital-first" consultancies, and LinkedIn gurus peddling "10x ROI" like it's kombucha. Oh, the Clickocracy! A glittering pyramid scheme of futurists, growth hackers, and business press sycophants, all singing hymns to the algorithm. This cast of characters will sell you fairy tales about AI-powered unicorns and "hyper-personalization," while their conferences resemble tent revivals for the terminally online. ("Can I get an amen for the pixel tracker?!")

The point is the system is rigged to be incomprehensible. Clickocrats thrive on complexity, their entire empire built on a foundation of techno-babble and FOMO. "You don't understand programmatic bidding?" How quaint. They blur the line between marketing reality and virtual reality because it's all about digital, baby! Just hand over your budget and pray to the conversion gods. Their grand delusion? That digital marketing is a science, not a casino. That every click can be optimized, every human reduced to a data point. Sure, sometimes it works, if your product is as thrilling as a Netflix docudrama. But for the rest of us mortals, it's a hamster wheel of diminishing returns, dressed up as "innovation."

Yet the Clickocrats march on, unburdened by doubt. After all, reality never interferes with the cult. Later in this book, I'll share examples of digital-only companies, the people who are supposed to know and be good at the game, companies like Uber, that have gotten their ass handed to them.

So with Clickocrats at the helm, the digital marketing space will continue to grow for a variety of reasons that we'll discuss here, mainly, peer pressure. Yeah, peer pressure. Come on! Everyone is doing it. Of course, it doesn't matter that digital, or many aspects of it, may not be right for certain businesses, but with their paycheck tied to digital everything,

THE CLICKOCRACY

BIG TECH

- MARKETING INFLUENCERS
- BUSINESS MEDIA, BLOGS, NEWSLETTERS, PODCASTS
- MARKETING PROFFESIONALS

some Clickocrats can be crafty and persuasive when dealing with a largely under-educated market that longs for growth, while others simply may not know better because they're busy running their businesses. Either way, the costs to businesses can be, and in many respects are, great. So, amidst confusion—manufactured confusion, I may add—along with denial, Clickocrats willingly and slavishly turn over their budgets, time, attention, and energy to their AdTech and social media overlords. What do they get in return? "Feeling better" about where they spent their marketing spend. Because, you know...everyone is doing it and, of course, analytics.

Like most things that impact our lives, follow the money. Clickocrats perpetuate the Clickocracy because their paychecks depend on it. Perhaps there's nothing more fitting to describe this phenomenon than Upton Sinclair's famous words, "It is difficult to get a man to understand something when his salary depends on his not understanding it." The Clickocracy's echo-chamber is essential to digital marketing's mythmaking. Recently the same people, institutions, and businesses who are key members of the Clickocracy have pivoted from social media to AI, but I'm not going down that rabbit hole right now. Clickocrats are led by "influencers" and digital industry hype people, some with real star power and followers by the millions. Of course, this couldn't be done without a compliant and adoring legacy media narrative that's digging its own grave in the process. Clickocrats with a wide following are happily platformed by business media, on TV and radio, as well as blogs and social accounts. To their mutual benefit, they cross-sell audiences, much like country music and rap collaborations.

By stage-presence alone, Clickocrats seem to convince CEOs, CMOs, and business leaders that the road to marketing nirvana is paved with content and clicks. They demand beaucoup bucks touting digital campaigns and tipping-points, profess the emanant success of everything digital like AI, swear by "smart-data" (no such thing, ever), and promote invented terminology like "brand authenticity," or "customer journey," which allows them to create a veneer of credibility and authority. Let me quickly take a left turn here to say customers don't go through journeys, but marketing thought-leaders seem to think so, with many businesses falling in line. So, they'll tell you with unmatched certainty that Coca-Cola, Nike, HBO, or your local pizzeria need to be authentic to be successful businesses and pay attention to their customer journeys. It's Friday night; I want a pizza. That's my journey. I need a new stove; I do my research; I buy a stove. That's my journey. Does authenticity mean making great products, delivering exceptional service, doing things to make people happy, and getting them to like your product? Is that authenticity? Adding more ingredients to the business word salad is nothing new; it becomes harder for people not to use them because they quickly become part of the lingo, so if people don't use them, they may feel like they're not part of the business culture.

The Death of Expertise (and How to Resurrect It)

Clickocrats' rise to power and prominence has contributed to the degradation of marketing expertise. But this didn't happen overnight. It was slowly suffocated by three myths:

1. **The myth of the "data-driven" messiah.** We've been sold the lie that data replaces intuition. But data is a rearview mirror; it tells you where you've been, not where to go. When Pepsi's Kendall Jenner ad flopped, it wasn't for lack of data; it was for lack of wisdom. Algorithms optimized for "engagement" told them controversy works. They didn't foresee the backlash because data can't measure cultural tone-deafness. True expertise lies in balancing analytics with anthropology. Take Liquid Death, the canned water brand that mocked sustainability clichés with heavy metal absurdity. Their CMO didn't rely on focus groups; they relied on counterculture intuition. Result? A $700 million valuation. Data informs; intuition innovates.

2. **The myth of the "self-service" marketer.** Platforms like Meta and Google have turned marketing into a DIY circus. "Anyone can do it!" they claim, offering drag-and-drop ad builders and AI copywriters. But democratization without education and experience breeds chaos. Middle managers with no marketing background now launch campaigns armed with LinkedIn hot takes and ChatGPT prompts, leading to disasters like Chevrolet's AI-generated Super Bowl ad, a cringe fest of stock footage and robotic voiceovers. Expertise isn't elitism; it's accountability. Just as you wouldn't let an intern perform surgery, you shouldn't let amateurs pilot brand strategy.

3. **The myth of the "hustle" mentality.** The cult of "growth hacking" has reduced marketing to a game of loopholes and shortcuts. Black-hat SEO, fake reviews, influencer fraud—these aren't tactics; they're symptoms of a profession losing its moral compass. When BMW was caught

stuffing car trunks with keyword-packed pamphlets to game search engines, they didn't "hack" the system. They revealed their desperation. Expertise means playing the long game. Look at REI's #OptOutside campaign. They closed stores on Black Friday, sacrificing short-term sales for a brand ethos that's paid dividends for a decade.

Digital Marketing's Original Sin: The Illusion of Control

Digital platforms seduced us with the promise of precision: "Track every click! Optimize every penny!" But this illusion of control has blinded us to three existential threats:

1. **The platform trap.** Marketers now rent audiences from tech oligarchs. When Apple's iOS 14 update gutted Facebook's tracking, e-commerce brands lost 30 percent of their targeting precision overnight. Those who'd built brand equity (like Patagonia) survived. Those reliant on hyper-targeted ads (like DTC fad brands) collapsed. Lesson: Own your audience or remain a digital serf.

2. **The creativity crisis.** Programmatic ads and AI-generated content have turned creativity into a commodity. Why craft a timeless tagline when you can A/B test 50 variations of "50% Off!!!"? But as Mark Ritson warns, "If your brand is built on price, you're one algorithm update from oblivion." Contrast this with Dove's Real Beauty campaign. Dove didn't just sell soap; it challenged societal norms. Decades later, it's still studied in business schools.

3. **The attention recession.** The average attention span is now 8 seconds, shorter than a goldfish's. Marketers respond by shouting louder: pop-ups, autoplay videos, click farms. But bombarding audiences isn't a strategy—it's surrender. Red Bull's Stratos Jump—a live-streamed space dive—didn't beg for attention. It *commanded* it by offering something rare: awe.

A Manifesto for Responsible Marketing

Everything that Clickocrats will tell you to do, do the opposite. To escape the digital dumpster fire, I've boiled it down to embracing five principles:

1. **Reject vanity metrics.** Likes, shares, and open rates are cocaine for the C-suite, addictive but hollow. Focus on *behavioral* metrics: repeat purchases, referral rates, and customer lifetime value. Example: Glossier's 90 percent retention rate isn't driven by Instagram likes, it's fueled by cult-like community-building and powered by offline strategies.

2. **Resurrect brand sovereignty.** Stop renting audiences from Zuckerberg. Build owned channels: email lists, podcasts, loyalty programs. Taylor Swift's decision to re-record her masters was a boss masterclass in owning her narrative.

3. **Rehumanize creativity.** Fire your AI copywriter. Hire poets. Apple's "Here's to the Crazy Ones" was written by a screenwriter, not a SEO bot.

4. **Reject growth at all costs.** Profitability and hustle culture are toxic. I know it's hard to hear, but permagrowth doesn't exist, so don't chase it. Basecamp's $3 billion valuation with zero VC funding proves slow growth can beat viral hype.

5. **Restore ethical guardrails.** If your tactic requires a Terms of Service loophole, it's not clever; it's corrupt. Remember when Volkswagen lied about emissions, they didn't "hack" regulations. They imploded their brand.

So step back, take a deep breath, and get back to basics. Marketing is full of bullshit, but its fundamentals will never let you down.

But Wait, There's More! (Act Now; Think Never!)

Oh, the miracles of modern marketing! We've traded the muse of creativity for the cold communion of data. Kneel before the altar of algorithms, where "innovation" means churning out more digital landfill, ads no one sees, posts no one reads, campaigns that vanish into the void like prayers to a server farm. And guess what? The junk pile grows taller by the second. While you read this sentence, another 10,000 brands just auto-posted AI-generated slop to LinkedIn. Congrats, you're witnessing the extinction of imagination in real time!

> **"The nose of a mob is its imagination. By this, at any time, it can be quietly led."**
>
> —Edgar Allan Poe

It was Mark Zuckerberg himself who in his May 2025 interview with Stratechery pulled the "trust me, bro" card. Zuck smugly waxed about removing agencies from the digital advertising process, at least on his platform, and said:

> We believe at this point that we are just better at finding the people who are going to resonate with your product than you are. And so, there's that piece. But there's still the creative piece, which is basically businesses come to us and they have a sense of what their message is or what their video is or their image, and that's pretty hard to produce and I think we're pretty close.

He went on to say:

> ...we're going to get to a point where you're a business, you come to us, you tell us what your objective is, you connect to your bank account, you don't need any creative, you don't need any targeting demographic, you don't need any measurement, except to be able to read the results that we spit out. I think that's going to be huge, I think it is a redefinition of the category of advertising. So if you think about what percent of GDP is advertising today, I expect that that percent will grow. Because today, advertising is sort of constrained to like, "All right, I'm buying a billboard or a commercial..."[1]

Trust me, bro.

Here's what's really scary: there are many people, including the old Clickocrat clan, who are blindly cheering this on. This is coming from a guy who said his company is going to create digital friends, meaning fake people, to connect and interact with real people—the same guy whose company says it purges about 1 billion fake Facebook accounts per quarter...and some people are cheering this on? Look, I'm not saying this stuff isn't going to happen. Lord knows, these people have successfully sold BS many times, but this takes the cake. No need to think about your business, products, budgets, or anything like that; just hand over your bank account to Facebook. They got this.

> **"Because we cannot measure the things that have the most meaning, we give the most meaning to the things we can measure."**
>
> —Fred Hargadon

Let's move on to creativity. But that's for *artists*, right? Today's marketers are glorified button-pushers, judged not by their ideas, but by their ability to grovel at the feet of Meta's latest "innovation." Spoiler: It's just another way to spy on your customers. The Clickocrats cheer, "Why think when you can automate? Why strategize when you can outsource your brain to Google or ChatGPT?" Hand over your budget, your dignity, and your common sense. They'll spin it into a "targeted campaign" that's 100 percent trackable, 0 percent impactful, you'll love it...trust me, bro. Just keep giving these people your money and everything will be fine. But here's the kicker: the machines may be good at this, but the people who operate them aren't even good at this...yet. The machines are fast and the people are slow. So using digital tools, some marketers have become faster at flooding the world with disposable content, faster at burning cash, faster at reducing marketing to a game of "Who can repurpose a TikTok trend quickest?" The Clickocrats don't care. They've got KPIs to hit, conference panels to keynote, and a universe of digital junkyard to keep expanding. So go ahead, feed the beast. Creativity was overrated anyway, no?

Most certainly, digital makes it easier, and perceivably cheaper, for businesses and marketers who want to justify every dollar spent and link that spending to analytics. Businesses have the absolute right to expect that of any platform. Let's be fair though: digital marketing works for many businesses—it has delivered and continues to—but not without many incredibly glaring holes I've already discussed in the previous pages.

A Gartner's 2024 marketing study showed 87 percent of marketing executives reported problems with campaign performance in the past 12 months, and 45 percent report possibly terminating a campaign early due to poor performance.[2] But what I can't figure out, because I genuinely don't know, is whether these campaigns were truly failing or whether there were internal pressures that have led these folks to pull the plug as a result of short-term thinking driven by everything digital.

The appetite for everything digital marketing continues to be insatiable and unrelenting. In the coming pages, we'll explore the dangers of digital marketing, because it has and continues to prove itself inefficient and alarmingly expensive. I'll also outline how marketing digital side of the house becomes a blind spot that is rarely challenged, not because there isn't a well-established case, but because it's often overwhelmed by the Clickocrat mob. Well-meaning marketers, by and large, are anesthetized, beaten into submission, addicted to and paralyzed by the drug that is digital marketing because of its promise, however illusive, to make marketing more effective, easier, and "cheaper." Finally, we'll explore other channels in an effort to show readers the value of integrated marketing.

2 Don't Hate the Player. Hate the Game.

Who can blame Clickocrats? They've got a right to make a living, plus they've got numbers on their side. A June 2024 study of U.S. adults by eMarketer showed average time spent on media per day was split into 64 percent on digital media and 36 percent on traditional media, and that gap is projected to be wider in 2025 and 2026.[3] When I shared the study on LinkedIn, a commentor said, "Fish where the fish are!" He's not entirely wrong, but I would characterize that comment akin to boiling down basketball to shooting threes, dunks, and blocked shots. A dumbed-down, unrealistic view, albeit feel-good view of the game. That's the point though: people get excited and emotional about digital media.

We're told by Big Tech that all their bells and whistles empower businesses, yet what we have today is a much narrower idea of marketing because people have less media options. As of April 2024, 94 percent of Americans are online according to Forbes[4] and about 80 percent of those use Google as their search engine, while daily newspaper circulation went from an approximate 56 million in 2000 to 21 million in 2022.[5] The number of pay TV customers has been slashed in half from about 100 million in 2013 to 56 million in 2024.[6] So yeah, fish where the fish are. Our mobile devices have become our life. For many, mobile devices have become an essential gateway to their health and well-being. Sleep apps or counting steps? That's so 2018. Today your phone or watch can read your heart rate, address mental health issues, or alert diabetics to their blood glucose levels. It's safe to say that a good portion of our lives and even well-being are now connected to the cloud in one way or another.

Big Tech understands better than anyone our visceral connection to devices and our digital addiction. Hell, they created and perpetuated it and continue to do so with no end in sight. From lightbulbs and refrigerators, self-driving cars to home heating systems, there's nothing Big Tech doesn't grasp. But implanting technology alone won't guarantee Big Tech's control on our lives now and going forward. To cement its central role in our lives, Big Tech spends hundreds of millions, a pittance, on lobbying governments in the U.S. and around the world. Lobbying efforts are designed to keep regulators confused, in a constant state of chasing changing technologies. Take Google, for example, who paid over $1.5 billion in fines and settlements in the United States alone since 2011, against a market cap of $2.2 trillion at the time of writing these words. Chump change for no change. Regulators are trying to catch up to Google and Big Tech, but with their unprecedented, prominent presence at the inauguration of President Trump, I doubt there could be much movement or inclination to address the concerns of business and consumers. So, if the old saying in Washington D.C., "personnel is policy" holds, Google will continue business as usual. I encourage you to check out some of the testimonies of the world's largest tech companies in front of various government bodies in the U.S. and around the world. Fueled by piles of cash and over-the-moon stock prices, Big Tech has successfully built a self-sustaining ecosystem whose principal function is to protect and grow its business. A good chunk of that ecosystem is comprised of but not limited to marketing technology companies, AdTech and digital marketing companies, mainstream media outlets, marketing influencers, and "thought leaders." These entities, each in its own way, work to shape the taste and direction of Clickocrats who perpetuate Big Tech's dominance within their own companies and industries to keep their people in line and money machines well-greased to ensure they dominate every key stroke in every

I CREATE CONTENT ABOUT CONTENT MARKETING FOR CONTENT MARKETERS MARKETING TO OTHER CONTENT MARKETERS.

ME TOO!

TOM FISH BURNE

industry: marketing, airlines, food retailers, sports, primary education—every industry.

We live in an era where the appearance of expertise has become accepted expertise, the loudest and most confident voices get attention. These thought leaders or cheerleaders profit handsomely. Some have built empires from thinly veiled everything digital. At the same time, with dangerous consequences that defy ethics and business sense, the Big Tech Clickocracy cabal has successfully managed to silence their critics by overwhelming them with the sheer volume of their output across platforms, digital and legacy, creating virtual conformity across industries, including marketing. Those who dare to speak out, like Lina Khan, Commissioner of the United States Federal Trade Commission for example, are harassed by Big Tech billionaires. Or Elon Musk suing his critics into silence as in the case of GARM, the Global Alliance for Responsible Media,[7] an industry association of advertisers on online platforms, and some of its members specifically, for declining to purchase ads on Musk's website.

Big Tech's control over the lives of billions has never been more pervasive, and its influence will continue to grow. In the case of social media, it's never been clearer that the platform is the message. Social media's meteoric rise has come to transform and shape how humans think, believe, and interact. What Big Tech wants is undying and unwavering compliance and conformity in the digital space. Remember marketing is only one of many profit centers for a lot of these digital companies. It's to their advantage to create conditions that paint those who have a different perspective, however valid and reasonable, as fringe. It's safe to say that marketing today is so tightly married to AdTech that it may literally be physically uncomfortable for marketers to think about other marketing channels.

Digital Delusion

Digital marketing's ultimate allure is the promise of an unprecedented sense of control and efficiency in marketing advertising. At its core, digital marketing allows businesses to find customers on the cheap (painting with broad strokes here). The fundamental idea that you can select and reach an audience—based on specific characteristics and certain social and behavioral profiles—and track results is truly remarkable, even today. Analytics providing a gateway to clicks, visits, open rates, likes, and shares have become the definitive choice to marketers today who convince themselves, through digital marketing, that they can bend the will of customers to their whims regardless of economic conditions. They will outright dismiss that Facebook, for example, has reported showing ads to more people than are alive, or Google may serve ads to fake websites that no human ever visits while counting the very same fake sites and visitors as real. In this frenzy, these marketers often lose sight of their customers' humanity and the connection to their product and service. Humans indeed are fickle creatures, ripe with self-interest, who live in a world of macro events that can't be tamed by marketing, digital or otherwise. None of this matters to Clickocrats. There are times, many times, when humans don't want to buy anything today or for the foreseeable future. But don't tell that to the digital marketing crowd.

Don't mistake pragmatism for piety. At Verasoni, we wield digital tools like scalpels, not crutches. Yes, we deploy algorithms, ads, and analytics, but without the cultish devotion that turns marketers into sycophants. Let's be brutally honest: marketing isn't magic. It's mud, sweat, and the occasional miracle. We don't coddle clients with fairy tales about viral jackpots; we drag them into the trenches, where failure is fertilizer and transparency is oxygen, making for better outcomes and stronger brands. I get it: marketers cling to data like a life raft. After years of clients screaming, "Why aren't we trending?!" or "Why aren't we getting enough website traffic?!" who wouldn't hide behind a dashboard? But here's the deadpan truth: digital platforms didn't just disrupt marketing; they lobotomized it. They turned strategists into screen-zombies, fixated on metrics that measure everything except meaning. Today's "campaigns" are fire-and-forget missiles launched by button-pushers, their creators hunched over analytics like day-traders chasing a penny stock's heartbeat. This isn't marketing. It's malpractice.

Judgment is the real casualty here. Judgement is what makes Steph Curry so good because he knows how to get the shot he wants. In marketing, judgement is forged by wrestling with budgets, sniffing out cultural shifts, and knowing when to ignore the data and the people who know your job better than you. Digital's seductive ease has atrophied that muscle, replacing instinct with a Pavlovian addiction to immediacy.

But Verasoni's rebellion is simple: we treat platforms as tools, not temples. No delusions. No genuflecting. Just grit, guts, and the gall to ask, "What happens when the Google's algorithm breaks or changes, when Instagram and email is down, and all you've got left is your brain?"

> **"The other complication is that the larger the advertiser the more likely they have handed their multimillion dollar budgets to media agencies to spend. Even if the agency is knowledgeable and means to do the right thing, they are not incentivized to look too closely for fraud. In fact, they are incentivized to not look, unless the client insists."**
>
> —Anonymous CMO in conversation with Dr. Augustine Fou[8]

Marketing Basics Are Exciting if You Pay Attention

Fundamentally, marketing is simply a communication lever businesses use to grow. To the extent it can make an impact, marketing is simply a tool that solves a business problem. Nothing more, nothing less. It's about how businesses or people convince people to buy their stuff (products, services, ideas) and keep them buying. Yet no business or snake oil merchant can sell their products, services, or ideas if they cannot articulate their value and appeal to their buyers. Things and ideas don't sell themselves. If your business or idea is a sports car, marketing is fuel.

At its core, marketing is an ancient pact between human desire and human ingenuity. People don't just "buy stuff." They seek solutions, stories, and symbols that resonate with their fears, aspirations, and identities. The transaction is merely the endpoint of a deeper dialogue: How does this product make me feel seen? How does this service quiet my uncertainty?

Yet in today's fractured attention economy, this dialogue has become a shouting match. Platforms splinter audiences into fragments; algorithms prioritize speed over substance. For marketers today, the challenge isn't just cutting through noise, it's redefining what "cutting through" even means. Are we crafting moments of genuine connection? Are we perpetuating distraction or earning trust?

The paradox is this: the human attention span appears to be shrinking. The more channels we have to reach people, the harder it becomes for our products, services, and ideas to matter to them. A vase sold on Instagram, software demoed on LinkedIn, a vacation pitched via TikTok, all must answer the same unspoken question: why would anyone pay attention to this, and why now, at this very moment? Not because the buyer is overwhelmed, but because they're weary. Weary of hollow personalization, of brands that confuse "targeting" with understanding. In August 2024, CNN reported "the average focus time for individuals looking at a singular screen dropped from 2.5 minutes in 2004 to an average of 47 seconds in 2021, according to Dr. Gloria Mark, a professor of informatics at the University of California, Irvine, and author of *Attention Span: A Groundbreaking Way to Restore Balance, Happiness and Productivity.*" The same article went on to quote D. Graham Burnett, the founder and director of a nonprofit dedicated to attention activism, the Institute for

Sustained Attention, and cocreator of the Strother School of Radical Attention in Brooklyn, New York, who calls this the "commodification of our attention." Burnett, who is also the Henry Charles Lea Professor of History at Princeton University in New Jersey, went on to say, "The market has priced our attention by competing in an 'attention economy' that's influencing the internet, social networks, and our lifestyles. Our attention is being monetized as never before…. We are living through a kind of gold rush, a gigantic technologically intensive and heavily capitalized program of financial exploitation of our most intimate and fundamental attentional capacities."[9] Yeah, human attention span is getting closer and closer to the attention span of a goldfish, which is reported to be about 8 seconds. Good job, everyone!

Reduced attention span makes marketing more challenging. Before you can persuade a customer, you must capture attention and their imagination. This is especially true for new brands, personalities, and ideas. From there, marketers have to move customers to persuasion, and that happens when brands deliver meaning along with the product or service. It's recognizing that the initial purchase, depending on the product and situation, could be a vote of confidence in a world of infinite options. Once we grab attention, we must hold it with integrity and continue to foster that relationship (assuming we're dealing with a long-term relationship and not a transactional brand). To "move people to buy," we must leave them feeling moved and satisfied, not manipulated. No one wants a used car dealer experience, whether it's in a physical or digital store. The best brands do this without losing sight of their humanity, or that of their customers. Because when the platforms fade and the trends collapse, the irreducible truth remains: people buy what's meaningful to them. So, your brand story must matter to your customers as much as the quality of your products, services, or ideas.

At its best, marketing is mythmaking that pulls in and captivates its audience and gets them to do what the seller wants. Though no one wants to feel manipulated, marketing is manipulation. It's nudging, reminding, pleading, teaching, and sometimes just showing up. Seasoned marketers do it with clarity, creativity, and simplicity, with the aim of winning hearts and minds.

Pet Rock's success in the mid-1970s was about a simple idea. Classical economics where the rational consumer decides to buy based on economic interest was thrown out the window. Who in their right mind would buy a rock? Yet, Pet Rock struck gold by being at the right place at the right time, with a captivating story that resonated with people and moved them to buy. Would Pet Rock have succeeded today? During the Great Depression? I'd bet against it. So, what products like Pet Rock demonstrate is that the time element of "when is your product" or "when is your brand" are just as important to the product and its marketing strategy as the story around it. Many products that enjoy success today would likely not have had success if they showed up at a different time. Lululemon would not have succeeded in the 1970s because the macro-economic situation at the time, along with other critical socio-economic factors, were different. Yet the essential lessons of Pet Rock and Lululemon are people fell in love with both ideas, which happened to be right for their time.

The "when" is your brand is rarely discussed, if not ignored. Yet timing is an important part of the calculus of any campaign. Campaigns are inextricable from the time in which they're conceived and rolled out. They live in the moment with all the things that are happening around them: extreme weather, oil market jolts, layoffs, and so on. If your campaign builds on past campaigns, you may have both data and experience on your side. Perhaps macro events may have changed since your last campaign, which can impact your next one. Have consumer preferences or appetites changed for products or services like yours? Supply chain issues affecting your product or sector? Are there viable alternatives or have competitors dropped from the market creating opportunities to fill in the void? Seasonality? Do you need to change your price? Understanding "when" in your campaign is more important than ever because trends, tastes, and markets change faster today than ever before. It's worth it to take a little more time to ask questions and include "when" in campaign planning.

In 2021, Apple sent a seismic earthquake when it changed its privacy policies, requiring third-party mobile apps to ask for permission when they want to track users across apps and websites owned by other companies. If you launched email campaigns soon after Apple's changes, you may have noticed your open rates drop to the bottom of the ocean. If you were informed, you would have segmented your audience by device or even email client (if possible) and would have noticed that open rates for Apple mail users were perhaps comparable to previous campaigns and created estimates for non-Apple mail users. Apple's privacy push also crushed Facebook's abilities to track users, so if you're running Facebook campaigns, you'll find a significant drop in campaign performance because Apple, in effect, has limited your reach to its devices. Were you taken by surprise or prepared when Apple made these changes? How fast did you revise your campaign?

From busy bazars along the Silk Road, to the shops of the Ming Dynasty in Beijing, to the e-commerce frenzy of today, marketing a business has always been fraught with seen and unseen risk, though as I mentioned earlier, never in the history of marketing has it become more complicated and chaotic since Big Tech came on the scene. Only a few will admit that the promise of digital marketing to make it easier, more effective, efficient, and personalized has not fully materialized. Of course, digital marketing has opened markets, created opportunities, and delivered customers. One could argue more broadly that for many businesses, digital marketing got a bigger portion of offline shoppers to online, but the pie didn't become bigger. But the real winners of the digital marketing game are Big Tech companies and the digital ad market makers and toll providers who get paid and rewarded for every transaction regardless of success or failure. Yet those who are pushing for everything digital, like Amazon, Apple, Uber, and the like, continue to take strong position in legacy media like television, direct mail, billboards, and so on.

Those who are closely following the narrow orthodoxy of digital marketing may not recognize nor admit that it has become an unwelcome, oppressive, and wasteful tax on businesses. Those who do, like yours truly, are considered party poopers. Party poopers like me know marketing today is about as easy and efficient as drinking water from a fire hydrant inside a vacuum cleaner while being attacked by killer bees. We also want to bring some semblance of sanity back to this profession. So how do marketers step back, take a breath, and develop marketing plans and campaigns that make business sense in the face of this noise and pressure? How do they absorb the hits coming from marketing geniuses and futurists and avoid doing the costly bidding of Big Tech?

I remember meeting with one of the largest consumer brand companies in the world who discovered, with our help, their products backed by a strong brand could translate well into the B2B healthcare space in the U.S. They boasted a dominant presence in other spaces but little exposure in their next venture. Armed with a shoestring budget and a B2B sales team with little marketing experience, the vice president of sales demanded to see a plan on how we can "create a movement" to get B2B customers to buy paper towels and toilet paper and do it digitally. While uttering "create a movement," he seemingly started levitating in the adoring eyes of everyone in the room. He was a visionary who knew something. While his underlings nodded in awe, I was recalling the incredible movements and communities around office cleaning products. Remember those? Yeah, me neither. When I asked about budget, he pointed me to the many viral campaigns he's heard of and wondered out loud, "Why can't we do that?" Everyone enthusiastically nodded in agreement as they eagerly awaited a precise response from me.

"Sadly, the real world has intruded on our fantasy world. In fact, there has never been a time when there has been more confusion, corruption, and misinformation about advertising. There has never been a time when advertisers chased rainbows, believed charlatans, and were taken to the cleaners by con men as they are now. And most of it is centered on online advertising—the very thing that was going to set us free."
—Bob Hoffman, former advertising executive,
from his book *Inside the Black Box*

Marketing Mascaraed

Every sector has its own echo-chamber, but marketing's echo-chamber is elaborately painted with frescos of beautiful bullshit stacked upon bullshit. We're all familiar with corporate lingo that looks for the lowest hanging fruit, circles back, and at the end of the day, either takes a deep dive

or put a stake in the ground. If there was an Olympic event in corporate speak or useless business jargon, marketers would win gold every time.

But it's not just invented terms; its categories like Millennials, Gen Z, and so on. Here's the thing: Gen Z, Millennials, Gen Xers, and Boomers are simply demographics. And yes, they can be coined as such to categorize them, but businesses have spent billions on research trying to understand the motivations of Millennials, as if they are a monolith. They send their people to conferences and webinars, and hire fancy consultants to understand just what makes this or that group tick. This is insane. Yet when you treat Millennials as a demographic, seasoned marketers know they can apply and deploy well-established demographic behavioral models and get to the same place with less hype and more focus and efficiency. The Millennial hysteria sure sold lots of conferences and scores of books, and made many people sound smart in meetings, but it lacked real substance. For the love of everything that is good on Earth and at the risk of yelling at clouds, it's a friggin' demographic. Visit your favorite marketing blog or business TV show to see the same frenzy for Gen Z right now.

Another element in the degradation of marketing is the rise of ubiquitous and overly enthusiastic marketing experts by literally everyone regardless of their experience or line of work. HR, operations, IT, CFOs, literally everyone is a marketing expert. This junior varsity contingent is made up of people who seemingly know very little about marketing but read blogs, engage in social media, and dream of writing compelling commercials and "viral" ads. I'm not a betting person, though if I were, I would bet people don't opine on law, accounting, or operations with same passion as they do on marketing. Everyone seemingly fancies themselves as a creative, and why not? I believe we are all creative in one way or another, but that doesn't make us marketers or effective communicators. Marketing is accessible because it's a part of our collective culture, because we are bombarded by it, and sometimes, when it's really special, we are touched by it personally and collectively. Accounting, operations, finance, law, and so on are not a part of our collective experience.

In 2019, just before COVID, we were working with a regional bank who wasn't convinced our email strategy and platform recommendation was right for them, even though it mirrored other banks' successful strategies, including well-known brands like Bank of America and Capital One. Why the skepticism? Because when they presented our research and strategy in their director's meeting, the HR leader, who commanded organizational sway, had reservations about our recommendation "Because I know other banks are using another system that's verified for banking use, and they've been using it for a while. These guys presented at the banking association conference last year. And they're Millennials." Because, you know, Millennials know "technology."

When we explained that we knew the system well and we didn't recommend it because of limitations, including outdated design options, an inefficient backend, and higher costs, the HR leader turned marketing tech stack expert demanded we set up a call with the company. From that moment, I had no doubt our recommendations were going up in smoke and this company would be selected as their email partner, regardless of our well-thought-out business case. Her good friend was using it at another bank, so naturally it must be right. And of course, don't forget the Millennial thing. Millennials know things. After a lengthy call and demo with the company and our client, we confirmed that many banks were indeed using this awful product. The call once again reinforced that the system was cumbersome, inflexible, and overpriced. Our client was on the call; they saw and heard the same things we did. Once again, we advised and warned that this product was inferior and its ubiquity in the regional banking space is a result of a paid sponsorship of the banking association rather than educated customers buying the product. Pure and simple, it was pay to play in a largely under-educated market on the

"Thank you, sir. May I have another?"

—Kevin Bacon in *Animal House*

subject. Just as the sun comes up in the East and sets in the West, this client disregarded our recommendation and went with the inferior system. Six months into their deal, the bank figured out they were overpaying for an underperforming system, and they could not get out of the three-year contract they signed. Literally everything we said would happen, happened. Culture and power ate sound business decisions for breakfast to the detriment of the business.

The next time you attend a conference, pay careful attention to what is being said on stage and by whom, and try to forget the stage altogether. Notice that some of these marketing luminaries will tell you what to do, but not how to do it. Here's why: marketing results, across industries, are not as replicable as many would have you believe because marketing campaigns, successful or otherwise, occupy a certain time, space, and culture whose tactics may be duplicated but results can't be replicated. However, we can learn from the experiences of campaigns and replicate and tweak elements that can be used in our own marketing concoction. I will provide many examples later in this book.

Marketing Serfdom

While brands pour immense resources into organic social media and digital efforts, much of this activity is likely generating far more value for the platforms themselves—Meta, Google, TikTok—than for the businesses footing the bill. Just look at the stock charts. Big Tech's influence has lured companies into a Faustian bargain: in exchange for global reach and hyper-targeting, brands unwittingly feed the very systems that profit from their addiction to visibility. The consequences are staggering. Beyond the billions wasted on ineffective campaigns, these platforms have amplified societal fractures, polarizing discourse, exacerbating mental health crises, enabling exploitation, and embedding fraud into the digital ecosystem.

Yet, to dismiss technology's value would be shortsighted. Digital tools *have* revolutionized commerce, connected billions, and birthed innovations that redefine human potential. For marketers, the challenge isn't to abandon these tools but to wield them with ruthless and dispassionate discernment. By confronting the pitfalls, addiction-driven algorithms, opaque metrics, and ethical blind spots, businesses can transform digital marketing from a costly gamble into a scalpel-sharp asset. The path forward demands accountability, and it's certainly easier said than done: leveraging AI and data not for mindless engagement but for genuine connection, ethical storytelling, and measurable impact. And oh, this path isn't for every brand. It may or may not be right for you. To illustrate this balance, let's examine brands that turned social media into a force for growth without compromising their values, and how their strategies can be replicated.

Glossier
- **Strategy**: User-generated content and influencer marketing
- **Approach**: Glossier encouraged their customers to share their experiences on social media, leading to a massive amount of user-generated content. They also collaborated with micro-influencers, who shared authentic reviews and tutorials, creating a community-driven marketing approach.
- **Result**: Glossier's sales exploded, with the brand quickly growing into a multi-million-dollar beauty company.

Daniel Wellington
- **Strategy**: Influencer partnerships
- **Approach**: Daniel Wellington used Instagram influencers extensively to promote their watches. By providing influencers with discount codes to share with their followers, they created a sense of exclusivity and urgency.
- **Result**: This strategy led to significant growth, turning Daniel Wellington into a globally recognized brand with over 6 million watches sold.

Gymshark

- **Strategy**: Social media engagement and content creation
- **Details**: Gymshark built a community on social media by regularly engaging with their audience and sharing fitness content. They used influencers and brand ambassadors to promote their products and create buzz around their fitness gear.
- **Result**: Gymshark's sales skyrocketed, leading to its valuation at over $1 billion.

MVMT Watches

- **Strategy**: Facebook ads and Instagram marketing
- **Approach**: MVMT Watches focused heavily on targeted Facebook and Instagram ads, showcasing their stylish, affordable watches. They also used high-quality visuals and customer testimonials to build trust and attract attention.
- **Result**: MVMT grew from a crowdfunding campaign to a company generating millions in revenue and was eventually acquired by Movado for $100 million.

Fenty Beauty

- **Strategy**: Inclusivity and viral marketing
- **Approach**: Fenty Beauty launched with a wide range of foundation shades, which resonated with a diverse audience. They used social media to showcase real customers using their products, creating viral moments and building a loyal customer base.
- **Result**: Fenty Beauty made $100 million in sales within its first 40 days.

Pura Vida Bracelets

- **Strategy**: Cause marketing and social media ads
- **Approach**: Pura Vida Bracelets built a brand around a cause, donating a portion of their sales to charity. Facebook and Instagram ads targeted customers who were passionate about the causes they supported and encouraged social sharing.
- **Result**: This approach led to massive growth, with Pura Vida becoming a multi-million-dollar company.

The success of many businesses and personalities in the digital realm should be celebrated, but two things can be true at the same time. There are serious issues with digital marketing; these are demons that every business must face. For example, in June 2023, the Association of National Advertisers (ANA) published a "first look" study about waste and fraud in digital media and said, "The current programmatic media ecosystem is 'rife with waste' to the tune of $13 billion and maybe as much as $20 billion according to a new study by the Association of National Advertisers." Juniper predicts ad fraud will grow from $44.3 billion in 2024 to $107 billion in 2029. Integral Ad Science (IAS) says that in total between 30 percent and 50 percent of display ads are "non-viewable."[10] "Non-viewable" means the ad loads outside the screen's viewable area, the ad doesn't render in time for a viewer to see it, multiple ads are stacked on one another, or one of several other factors.

As reported in the *Wall Street Journal*, Google's YouTube ad deliveries onto third party sites through Google's video partners program violated Google's own terms of service with those advertisers. The study determined that an extraordinary number of videos and deliveries were delivered to sites where the video was either unviewable (invisible) or where the sound was off. The study added that videos were delivered to many sites that were dynamically generated only to carry ads, meaning fake and irrelevant sites or apps.[11] Soon after, in a MediaPost commentary, ad industry veteran and tech investor Dave Morgan lamented, "As many in our industry have been saying...we're an industry rife with willful ignorance...so many folks are making so much money, pushing budgets downstream and taking cuts as the money passes, the last thing they want is to know where the ad ended up, actually ran, and how many rules were broken in between."[12] A study conducted by Adalytics found that "For years, significant quantities of TrueView skippable in-stream ads, purchased by many different brands and media agencies, appear to have been served on hundreds of thousands of websites and apps in which the consumer experience did not meet Google's stated quality standards. For example, many TrueView in-stream ads were served muted and auto-playing as out-stream video or as obscured video players on independent sites. Often, there was little to no organic video media content between ads, the video units simply played ads only."[13] According to the *Wall Street Journal*'s coverage,

131 brands including Samsung, Disney+, Johnson & Johnson, E&Y, Microsoft, McDonald's, Zillow, Adobe, and TikTok (yep, you read that right) "may have purchased muted, auto-playing, mis-declared TrueView skippable in-stream inventory," as well as government entities including the Social Security Administration, the U.S. Army, and Medicare. The study also cited 10 media agencies and media buying companies that appeared to have transacted muted, auto-playing, out-stream TrueView ads including Interpublic Group (Matterkind, Initiative, Mediabrands), Dentsu (Amnet), Publicis (Audience on Demand, Precision), Omnicom (Accuen), WPP (Xaxis, Headlight, Essence), Havas (Affiperf), Jellyfish, Brain Labs Digital, Horizon Media (Canvas WorldWide), and MiQ.

These are not insignificant companies who lack budgets and marketing talent. If we put the agencies aside for a bit, one can easily argue TikTok, Microsoft, Samsung, and Disney+ are digital companies who should be experienced and savvy enough in this space to identify and avoid this type of fraud, no? Plain and simple, they should know what they're doing. So, if this can happen to iconic digital brands with talent and money, imagine what's happening to the rest of the business world—and not just on YouTube. On July 8, 2023, the *Financial Times* reported that UK Finance, which "represents more than 300 financial companies" said in a letter to Chancellor Jeremy Hunt that 61 percent of all reported "authorized push payment fraud by volume is connected to Meta, the company that owns social media sites Facebook, Facebook Marketplace, Instagram, and WhatsApp."[14] Not surprisingly, as I write these words, both Google and Meta have denied or refuted these reports.

We need a meaningful conversation about reframing marketing to separate the industry's seemingly irresistible sizzle reel of bullshit from the reality for every business of any size. Facebook and Google aren't just conglomerates; they are political forces with seasoned lobbyists at their beck and call. In late 2007, I told a friend that "It's clear that Zuckerberg is running a continent, not a social media site." Twelve years later, in 2018, he hired Nick Clegg, former Deputy Prime Minister of the United Kingdom and longtime Member of Parliament, as its vice president of global affairs and communications. In 2022, Clegg became President for Global Affairs. Coincidently, in March 2018, the *Guardian* reported Mark Zuckerberg refused to testify three times in front the UK's parliamentary committee investigating fake news. In 2019, Zuckerberg and his second-in-command, chief operating officer Sheryl Sandberg, skipped a subpoena by the Canadian Parliament to testify on similar issues. In February 2021, Facebook blocked news to all of Australia because the Aussies proposed a law that would force it to pay news publishers for displaying their content. They eventually cut a deal five days later where both Facebook and Australia claimed victory. The point is, Meta is more powerful than many countries on the planet and isn't afraid to challenge governments.

On May 15, 2025, the *Wall Street Journal* published an article with the sub-headline "Fake puppies and phony offers of mouthwatering bargains are often seeded by overseas crime networks; employees say company is reluctant to impede its advertising juggernaut." The article stated that Meta, the parent company of Facebook and Instagram, is "a cornerstone of the internet fraud economy" and "accounted for nearly half of all reported scams on Zelle for JPMorgan Chase between the summers of 2023 and 2024." The piece went on to say:

> Because of a safe harbor in U.S. telecommunications law known as section 230, platforms are generally shielded from liability for user-created content. Whether those protections apply to Meta's ads is now being tested by Andrew Forrest, an Australian mining billionaire and philanthropist who became frustrated in 2019 with Meta's failure to remove fraudulent investment advertisements using his image and AI-cloned voice. In a motion to dismiss the case last year, Meta argued that it is under no obligation to require investment advertisers to verify their identities or demonstrate that they're licensed to sell such products.[15]

This stuff is widely documented in the media and by consumer and business advocates. But Meta and its Big Tech peers continue to forge forward with impunity.

So, it's not a stretch to say Big Tech players operate with impunity, because they do. The cherry on top is businesses continue to blindly feed the Big Tech beast. Their impact on every aspect of our lives is profound in so many ways, from changing our politics to our social habits. No corner of humanity has been unaffected. Big Tech is a fierce political animal that understands election cycles, who's in power, what motivates them, and how to maneuver within and around the systems of government just enough to stay ahead of legislatures. It may sound ominous, but the reality is that the heads of these companies are heads of state with real economic and political ecosystems with billions of people and dollars at their command. Who was front and center at President Trump's second-term inauguration? Not past American presidents, or notable public servants, but the CEOs of Amazon, Facebook, OpenAI, Google, and so on. Still, regardless of how these companies behave politically, you'd think businesses who take pride in being super-efficient, data-driven, fierce negotiators would not succumb to vanity analytics and industry hype. The truth is business chooses easy over hard every time, even when easy works against its interest. But we've seen this established model work extraordinarily well in politics where people vote against their own interest and it's well-translated here.

But Will the Clickocracy Repent? (Spoiler: LOL, No.)

Ah, yes—the *astonishing* cases of fraud, waste, and digital snake oil will surely shake marketers' devout faith in their beloved tech! Any day now, they'll abandon their algorithmic altars, clutch their pearls, and return to the pure, untainted land of...oh wait, they won't. Because the grift is the point.

Let's marvel at the cognitive dissonance: marketers gasp at headlines about bot farms siphoning billions, then pivot straight to their daily ritual of dumping piles of cash into the same black boxes. "But the metrics and KPIs!" they whimper, as if trackable fraud is somehow nobler than the untrackable kind. Big Tech capitalizes on the truth: marketers are just dopamine junkies with expense accounts. Feed them a dashboard, a buzzword, and a sliver of hope, they'll keep lining up for their fix. And let's not forget the pièce de résistance: marketing automation, the Clickocracy's favorite fairy tale. Clients still ask, wide-eyed, "How do we automate our way to relevance?" as if efficiency and efficacy means replacing creativity. The reality is automation doesn't automate marketing; it automates mediocrity. Go ahead, set up those drip campaigns! Outsource your soul to a

> **"It is difficult to get a man to understand something when his salary depends on his not understanding it."**
>
> —Upton Sinclair

CRM consultant! Hire three agencies to manage the automation that was supposed to save you time! *Do you feel the savings yet?*

As I mentioned several times, and I can't overstate this, everyone's in on it and Big Tech profits from confusion—except you. Agencies profit from complexity. The marketers profit from plausible deniability ("Look, the data said it would work!"). And the C-suite is too busy to notice they're paying for digital servitude.

Marketing automation, like digital marketing, isn't a tool; if not done right, it's simply another tax. A tax on time, talent, money, and sanity. A tax levied by a priesthood of tech bros and "growth hackers" who look at your business and customers as economic units of data. A tax that funds the illusion of control in a world where attention is the only currency that matters, and we're all bankrupt.

I'll say this out loud: despite Zuck's mutterings about AI marketing automation, the only thing "automated" here is the downward spiral. Real marketing still requires humans. And that's a hill I'll die on. There is a need for those pesky creatures with ideas and ethics. Are the tech overlords telling us mere mortals that AI will manage AI? Who asked for this? From my perch, I see the business community building better chains for its own captivity and at the expense of jobs. But by all means, scale on.

Google and Facebook: Scraping the Bottom of the Pan

Before we tackle Google, let's start with the internet itself, which has its own fundamental issues that impact all businesses. A study by Barracuda Networks, the internet security firm, which covered a period from January to June 2021, showed internet traffic was generated by humans 36 percent of the time, "bad bots" 39 percent of the time, and "good bots" 25 percent of the time, while isolating the major source of the bots to North America. Barracuda's 2023 study of the same timeframe in 2023 showed things improving a bit with 18 percent good bots, 30 percent bad bots, and the rest human traffic. There are other studies by reputable outfits showing smaller (42 percent, 50 percent, etc.) but still significant bot activity remains at the core of total internet traffic for now.[16] With AI in our midst right now, I suspect those numbers are much higher, and I predict they'll get much worse.

They are especially telling considering right now, and for the foreseeable future, humans, not bots, buy stuff. Imagine looking at Google Analytics, seeing favorable traffic, and trusting that number as legit human traffic. If we're marketing to what appears to be bots X percent of the time, then X percent of our dollars is not working for us, no? To put it bluntly, X percent of our marketing dollars and energy are wasted. Keep in mind that bots have the ability to both visit your website organically, which shows "traffic" to your website, and click on ads that drain your Google, major search, and social advertising budget.

There are so many issues with Google that I could easily double the size of this book and provide data to boot. Take, for example, Google relevancy of top results: only 41 percent of the top 10 search results meet the user's intent, according to WalletHub's study on credit card and banking queries. Or its biased results that lack transparency, with 34 percent of the relevant pages appearing in the top 10 results show only advertiser products to consumers, and 58 percent of them are not transparent about doing so. Yet "Google has known for years that significantly reducing quality would not hurt the business in a significant way," according to WalletHub,[17] which is citing a lawsuit by both the United States and the State of Colorado filed against Google on August 5, 2024. But let's not get sidetracked with all this about Google not being as efficient as businesses and tech evangelists would have you believe.

> "Google's search advertising monopoly allows it to tax businesses globally, extracting rents through opaque and unfair pricing."
>
> —*Wall Street Journal* op-ed on Google's ad practices (2021).

To be sure, digital ad fraud is a significant problem for digital advertisers. According to Statista's recent estimates, the cost of ad fraud is projected to be about $100 billion in 2023, with Google Ads accounting for a significant portion of this staggering number. Fake clicks and impressions using bots, malware, click farms, fake websites—there's no shortage of possible fraud risk in any digital advertising campaigns, including Google AdWords.

Here are a few ways to tell if there's bot traffic on your site:

- Mistimed visits. There are lots of visits to your site at 3:30 a.m. local time when people are usually asleep.
- Extra high page views. Was there a sudden interest in your business?
- Very high bounce rate or low session duration.
- Very high visits from irrelevant locations. Your business is in Pittsburgh, but you have lots of visits from Prague.

Google Analytics provides a way to "exclude all hits from known bots" but only if the source of the bot traffic can be pinpointed. I don't believe there's a bullet-proof solution to stopping bots, but you need to be aware of their impact so you can adjust your strategies appropriately. In addition, if not set up properly, Google Analytics can provide inaccurate or misleading data about website traffic and user behavior.

It's important to note that Google Analytics and Google Ad Analytics are two different channels that serve different purposes. Google Analytics tracks and reports website traffic and visitor behavior on your website, like how many people visit your site, where they come from, how long they stay, and which pages they visit. Google Ad Analytics is a tool that tracks and analyzes the performance of your Google advertising campaigns. It allows you to track the performance of your Google Ads campaigns and measure the return on investment. Provided it's set up correctly, Google Ad Analytics can track the number of visits, impressions, conversions generated by your ads, and the cost per click and cost per conversion.

One important issue with Google is it changes its customer service team every three months. Businesses that aren't spending millions a month never get to speak with a dedicated representative who understands or gets to know their business or sector to add real value, like how to best allocate advertising dollars on the platform. Instead, Google Ads' rotative account managers are there to alert you to how little you're spending and encourage you to spend more to get more "reach." That's been our experience since 2006. As for Facebook? Well, just try to get someone on the phone.

I want to be clear: Google is a terrific avenue for marketing, but not all Google strategies are equal, and as a result, you may or may not be getting the value you expect. At the same time, I am not saying you should shut down your Google strategy; that would be absurd. You simply need to be more skeptical of where your Google focus and budget are going and what you're spending on search engine optimization or search marketing relative to the actual humans you reach who may be interested in your stuff.

Say it with me: there's plenty of waste in Google ads, and there's plenty of fraud in Facebook ads. Bottom line here, you should also assume that a portion of your Google Ads dollars is going into a black hole of bots and algorithms and comes back in the form of clicks and site visits, which makes some people say, "Our campaign is working! We had 15,000 to our site last month and 2,000 clicked on our ads!" Did you reach humans or bots? If humans, were they the humans you intended? Digital advertising fraud is real, and one thing is for sure: it will continue to evolve even as I type these words, and marketers must keep up or keep getting fleeced. No one wants to pay for fake clicks and campaigns that don't reach real people. It's burning money, but it's also a contributor to opportunity cost and possible damage to your brand's reputation, because your ads may show up on unsavory sites.

I encourage you to be skeptical of your Google Analytics and Google Ads reports. Probe more and be more curious about the traffic of your internal team and any marketing firm you hire. If you don't know the right questions, follow people like Dr. Augustine Fou, a prolific writer and thinker on the subject. Remember, Google is not marketing nirvana. Sometimes using Google to promote your business is as pleasant and smooth as a root canal, even if you know what you're doing. This is about getting better as a marketer, so #GetBetter.

The Rise of AI and LLMs

I am writing at the dawn of Large Language Models like ChatGPT, DeepSeek, and their ilk. All of this is very exciting, of course, though I am reminded of 2006, when everyone was super excited about social media but had no clue what to do with it. I thought the easiest way to do this would be to go right to the horse's mouth to ask ChatGPT about its impact on marketing, and it came back with this:

> As an AI language model, ChatGPT has the potential to significantly impact marketing in several ways. Here are a few examples:
>
> 1. Personalized marketing: ChatGPT can analyze customer data and help marketers create personalized marketing campaigns. It can also engage with customers in real time, answering their queries and concerns.
> 2. Content creation: ChatGPT can help marketers generate content ideas, write product descriptions, and even generate complete articles or social media posts. This can save marketers a lot of time and resources.
> 3. Customer service: ChatGPT can provide customer support 24/7, responding to customer inquiries and providing information about products or services. This can improve customer satisfaction and reduce the workload for customer support teams.
> 4. Data analysis: ChatGPT can analyze customer data to identify patterns and trends, helping marketers make data-driven decisions. It can also help with predictive analytics, allowing marketers to anticipate customer behavior and adjust their strategies accordingly.
>
> Overall, ChatGPT can help marketers streamline their processes, improve customer engagement, and increase ROI. However, it is important to note that AI language models like ChatGPT are still in their early stages and may require additional training and development to fully realize their potential in marketing.

Fantastic! More questions. Who's the human that is guiding your marketing AI? What is their experience?

Our time and zeitgeist feel eerily like 2006 all over again. That was the year Facebook was born and, while many point to Google as a watershed moment for the world we live in, I am inclined to start in 2006 for a host of reasons. Social media has changed our world more profoundly than the cotton gin or printing press, in my opinion. It wasn't about finding stuff but connecting people and the world, and in the process, Facebook in essence built the largest, most connected nation on Earth—for good, bad, or otherwise.

While Verasoni was in its infancy, I took a little more than a year to study the new landscape, players, implications, and opportunities to level set my understanding of what's real and what's hype. The ideas in this book germinated from the scar tissue and learnings from those early years. That year of study has proven to be an excellent investment because it continues to pay hefty dividends for Verasoni's clients.

Yet here we are again.... Fast forward about 20 years and AI is quickly pushing our world in unexpected ways. ChatGPT launched in spectacular fashion in 2022, soon after it unexpectedly got its teeth kicked-in by Deepseek, and one can imagine competitors on the horizon who will likely replace both platforms or force them to change, much like Google did to Yahoo, Facebook to MySpace, and Netflix to Blockbuster. In the race to leverage AI, the question is no longer whether companies should adopt LLMs, but how they can do so in a way that aligns with their unique needs and goals. For many, the answer lies in building their own. So, like I did back in 2006, I put pen to paper (those do exist you know, and they work quite well!), and I took 2023–24 to study AI, the hype, potential, and realities. Here's where I see things are going with LLMs with implications for marketing.

1. Private LLMs and AI Will Ultimately Prevail

Why? Public LLMs are trained on vast amounts of publicly available data, but they are not designed to handle sensitive or proprietary information securely. When companies input confidential data, such as customer information, trade secrets, internal strategies, or even marketing brochures into a public LLM, they risk exposing that data to third parties. Many public LLMs retain user input to improve their models, which could lead to unintended data leaks or breaches. That means your business is consenting public LLMs to use your information as they please.

Much like every company having its own website or network, every company will have its private LLM and or AI agent(s). And just as websites and the digital brand experience are attached at the hip, AI, when done right, will attract clients and make them stickier. For industries like healthcare, finance, banking, and legal services, where customer data and privacy is paramount, relying on public LLMs should be a nonstarter. Public LLMs have their tentacles in any and every publicly available iota of information on the web. They learn from it and uses it at their whims, without regard to copyright or IP ownership. At least that's what's going on right now. On the other hand, companies can use private LLMs to keep out public LLMs, creating walled gardens, and tailor them to operate within a company's secure infrastructure, ensuring that sensitive data never leaves the organization's control while leveraging the power of AI.

2. Customization for Industry-Specific Needs

Public LLMs are general purpose tools designed to cater to a wide range of users and industries. While they are versatile, they often lack the depth and specificity required for niche industries or specialized tasks. For example, a pharmaceutical company may need an LLM that understands complex medical terminology, regulatory requirements, and drug development processes. A public LLM may struggle to provide accurate, context-aware responses in such scenarios. By developing its own LLM, a company can train the model on industry-specific datasets, ensuring that it delivers highly relevant and accurate output. This level of customization is impossible with off-the-shelf public LLMs. For example, AI will be integrated heavily into sales, especially on the B2B side putting customers more in control than ever before because customers will create buying agents who can find, source, and negotiate for products faster and more efficiently than ever.

3. Intellectual Property and Competitive Advantage

We live in a knowledge-driven and attention economy where intellectual property (IP) is a competitive advantage. Public LLMs are trained on publicly available data, meaning they are limited because they cannot provide insights or solutions that are truly unique to a company. Moreover, using a public LLM to generate content or strategies could inadvertently expose a company's IP to competitors. A proprietary AI, trained on a company's internal data for its stated purposes, can generate insights and solutions that are unique to the organization. This not only protects IP but also enables the company to leverage its proprietary knowledge to innovate and stay ahead of the competition.

4. Control Over Model Behavior and Outputs

Public LLMs are designed to be neutral and broadly applicable, which means they may not align with a company's specific values, tone, or brand voice. For instance, a company with a strict compliance framework may need an LLM that adheres to specific guidelines and avoids generating content that could lead to legal or reputational risks. With a proprietary LLM, companies have full control over the model's training data, fine-tuning, and outputs. This ensures that the model behaves in a way that aligns with the company's goals, values, and regulatory requirements. Again, brand implications are huge here.

5. Ethical and Regulatory Compliance

Marketers would do well to pay attention to how regulations or lack thereof can affect their AI strategies. As AI regulations evolve, companies are increasingly required to ensure that their AI systems are transparent, ethical, and compliant with local laws. Public LLMs, which are often opaque in their training data and decision-making processes, may not meet these requirements. China is leading the way here; the U.S. and Europe are laggards. A proprietary LLM allows companies to implement ethical AI practices, such as bias mitigation, explainability, and compliance with regulations like GDPR or CCPA. This level of control is essential for building trust with customers and stakeholders.

Facebook and Social Media

Social media sucks the air out of the room, but it's an important part of the marketing landscape and has its virtues and pitfalls.

It should not be a surprise to anyone that businesses and CMOs continue to pound the table on social media like it's 2006. They're now trying to figure out how to go viral on TikTok. Before that it was Instagram, before that Twitter and, of course, Facebook. "Insanity is doing the same thing over and over and expecting different results," a quote that's seemingly attributable to Albert Einstein, seems befitting here, because we're back at it with TikTok. Anyhow, social media marketing is pursued with the same vigor and seriousness as other marketing channels even though data shows it may not be as effective as they think. Who cares about that? Did you see what so-and-so did on their Reels? Just like Google, marketers like social media because they can measure it. Platforms like Facebook spit out reports about likes, engagement, and voila! This is supported by an army of agencies and freelancers who work like worker bees protecting the queen (Facebook) by feeding it. The more they feed it, the more stuff it spits out, the better everyone feels. Agencies shower their clients with vanity analytics and glorified monthly reports and swiftly point to dashboards that flash numbers in cool primary colors designed to produce just enough dopamine to lull clients into thinking their efforts are worthy.

Like SEO, social media is a favorite of marketing tourists who tend to harp on its platforms as a primary way to get their message and product out. We like to start with the basic question of "To whom are we posting and why?" A business may have 1,970 followers on LinkedIn, 1,964 on Facebook, and 913 on Instagram. They want us to create hashtags because "Hashtags drive traffic." We also ask how many of your followers are real, because Facebook, LinkedIn, Twitter, and Instagram suffer from the same issue that plagues almost everything digital: fake accounts and fake traffic. With every social media strategy, start by making sure accounts represent real people who are likely to be their customers. That takes diligence and time.

Fake accounts, like fake web traffic or fake Gucci bags, are a real issue. Facebook regularly purges fake accounts, according to its own reporting. While there are about 8 billion people on Earth, between 2017 and 2022, Facebook purged a staggering 29 billion fake accounts.[18]

Facebook: Fake Accounts Purged (In Billions)

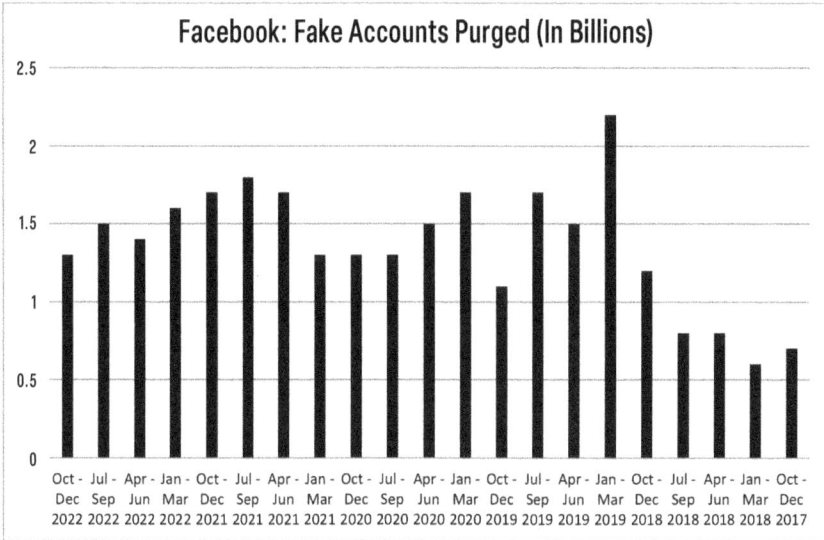

Yet, any practitioner worth their salt will point to relevant networks, not frequency or even quality of posts, though all three are important. If you don't have a relevant audience, who are you posting to, who are you engaging? In 2009, still early in Facebook's reign, I was invited to be a panelist at an entrepreneur conference in Parsippany, New Jersey, to talk about how business leaders can use social media to grow. The first question from the moderator was "Abe, can you tell us about how businesses can use free resources like Facebook to grow market share?" First, I addressed the false premise of the question, which the audience and moderator didn't appreciate: the "free" part. I responded by asking a few questions like "Which part of Facebook or any social platform is free?" I followed up by asserting "The time it takes to think about and create a business post is not free. The time it takes to build a network or community strategy is not free. The money and time it takes to hire and manage people to do your Facebook posts isn't free. What if your posts don't resonate? What if your graphics miss the mark?" Yet, this answer, which is evergreened to today, was summarily dismissed by the audience. None of these things seemed to matter to anyone there. The audience was pounding the table on Facebook as free marketing Christmas, and I was sourpuss Scrooge. In speaking with several attendees after the panel, they were puzzled by my position because they "know so many people on Facebook," and "so many businesses are on it." It's astonishing to see how businesses of all sizes have suspended disbelief and skepticism and have done so to their own detriment since 2007. Remarkably, that disposition is alive and kicking today as businesses continue to be gaslit by Big Tech. Now, it's TikTok.

We must acknowledge that social media has delivered in consequential and revolutionary ways for businesses. And since I believe we can live in a world where we can walk and chew gum at the same time, we need to look at what works and what doesn't in that space, because both coexist in the same universe. Major brands have won big with their scale and dollars powering complex digital and social marketing enterprises to reach and engage audiences. At the same time, small businesses like restaurants have successfully enticed diners with platforms like Instagram. Personalities seem to emerge out of nowhere to become world-wide stars, like Charli D'Amelio, who launched her channel in 2019, and now boasts a following of more than 103 million accounts.

It's interesting to note that when one scans the web or business literature looking for successful product launches or social media campaigns that have had a real impact, we don't find examples of small and middle market companies. Unsurprisingly, we find major brands like Apple, Nike, Starbucks, Oreos, and the like dominate the space. No one should be shocked here. Search results took me to industry pages that heaped praise on how these major business brands found social media success generating impressions or likes. So-and-so brand got 1,400 likes and 102,000 impressions. Are you kidding me? I have questions. If major brands can't find 1,400 accounts to like a post, then shame on them. How many of those likes and impressions were not human, meaning bots or fake accounts? What is the immediate or incremental benefit to these brands from these campaigns? Sales, brand recall, or...? How much did the campaigns cost in dollars and time? What, realistically, can smaller brands who have less money, power, and resources learn here?

Search for "best small business social media campaigns" as I did in November of 2024, and you won't find real answers. What you will find are marketing companies who sell social media services providing examples of mega brands like Nike, Oreos, Starbucks, and so on. So, it's totally predictable that major brands, armed with deep pockets, occupy the accolades on any platform if they choose, including social media. One would think that with all the data generated from social media posts and ads, we can easily find specific examples of how small business leveraged social media to grow. Of course, they are out there, but I am betting the kitchen sink that they are outliers.

Social media success starts with your network and community building strategy. Think of your social media channels, whether it's Facebook, LinkedIn, TikTok, or your email lists, as a television station in need of both programming content and audience. If there's no audience, you're broadcasting to no one.

Here are some social media facts I heed whenever I develop campaigns for clients:

- Your company works for social media sites, not the other way around. Your social team and agency efforts (cost = time + money + risk/reward) are traded for data that social sites use/sell.
- You do not own anything on social media. Not your content and more importantly not your network.
- Your network is more important than your content will ever be.
- Social media advertising is a black box. Facebook removes a billion fake accounts every quarter and your ad budget is in the hands of its algorithms and bots. Don't believe me? Google it.
- You should be on social media but understand how to use it for your best interest, not in the best interest of your digital agency, who will never have these conversations with you.
- For most brands, Twitter is about as useless as Elon Musk's hair transplant. So is Facebook. At the same time, social media is a necessary evil.
- The most important social media tool is...you ready? Email. Again, your agency will be silent here because "It's a lot of work."
- You must actively manage risks associated with social media. Social media for business is the riskiest of all media.
- Ask better questions about analytics and don't fall in love with dashboards. The entire digital marketing ecosystem is fraught with fraud. Know the incentives of your digital agency/partner.
- Your social media FOMO won't help you promote your business. Herd mentality around social media only adds to the potential and real waste in the space. Can I be frank here? I've

been all over this since 2006. Data upon data tells us social media is low yield/high cost, inefficient media. But this hype, based on a bunch of lies (no more Mr. Nice Guy because too many good businesses are being sideswiped in this mess) that get perpetuated by either paid, incompetent but well-spoken, or well-meaning "thought leaders" keeps the machine greased. CEOs don't understand the space and CMOs tell me that CEOs want to see analytics, so they keep feeding the machine, but it's also no wonder that many studies show that CEOs' trust in CMOs is low. If you think this is harsh and want to challenge this statement, please make sure you bring real data. I'll meet you anywhere, any time, and if you need a plane ticket, I'll buy it for you.

- Social media's risks must be actively managed because businesses have already wasted billions on this autopilot hot mess by good people in business.

- Final point: Businesses of all sizes mistake social media marketing as digital marketing. Not the same thing. Digital marketing, at this point in its lifecycle, is integrated marketing. Again, your digital agency and thought leaders, Clickocrats and their pals, will be silent on this because "It's not simple to sell."

I have always taken a pragmatic approach to marketing, building integrated plans that are married directly to business objectives, reviewing, measuring, and adjusting, while admitting there's room for failure in any campaign. Yet, there's one conundrum that continues to confound, and that's social media's outsized share of mindshare in business, namely Facebook.

Time and again, in our experience, including Verasoni's body of work since 2005, and in our research in the field, we have found Facebook to be one of the most inefficient organic marketing tools. In private conversations with CMOs and brands, they lament their frustration with Facebook but believe pressure from their boards, CEOs, peer groups in their firms, and industry prevents them from taking a more data-driven stance on the platform. Performative analytics happily dances on the grave of effective marketing.

So, What's Happening?

While organic Facebook strategies performed lower than expectations time and again, certainly in my experience, it continues to disproportionately receive attention and resource investment. What I've come to learn, and this is a theory, is that client expectations for Facebook and other social media platforms simply reflect the larger societal fascination with the idea of our connectedness. It reflects their own personal involvement on these platforms, be it as participants or as voyeurs. This attitude is especially pervasive in the middle market and small business environment.

Let's not forget the role of the social media industrial complex whose job is to perpetuate itself, and in the process, gaslights brands to "be content creators." This powerful force, along with a burning desire for vanity analytics, creates a powerful addiction to Facebook (and other platforms), effectively making every business and brand a serf and Facebook its master. Make no mistake about it: if your brand isn't looking at its Facebook positioning critically, your business is working mindlessly for Facebook and not for your business. Simply put, if you are posting organic content on Facebook either through your resources or an agency partner, your business is an unpaid volunteer content producer for Facebook.

> "Facebook's ever-changing algorithms force businesses into a pay-to-play model, squeezing small companies that can't afford rising ad costs."
>
> —Roger McNamee, early Facebook investor and critic, in *Zucked: Waking Up to the Facebook Catastrophe*

I consider Facebook, and other social media platforms, to be an added and wholly unnecessary tax on businesses that must be managed with a tight leash. The tax is not inconsequential. Like any tax, you want meaningful services in return. Businesses go out of their way to hire advisors to optimize their taxes; I would submit the same should go for Facebook because of its inefficiencies.

WHY ISN'T SOCIAL MEDIA MAGICALLY SOLVING ALL OF OUR PROBLEMS?

Just the Facts

Before COVID, P&G, the world's largest marketer, reduced its investment in digital/social. What do social media influencers think they know about "content development" that P&G doesn't? *Adweek* said, "When Procter & Gamble cut $200 million in digital ad spend, it increased its reach 10 percent."[19]

We are always going to come back to agility and efficiency in an integrated marketing environment. It's proven itself pre-COVID and thrust to the forefront post-COVID. From a digital perspective, the COVID experience has demonstrated that consumers want an entirely digital experience, not simply a buying channel. So, while Facebook, social, and digital remain important and must be part of every marketing portfolio, it's *how* businesses use them that really matters. They are tools within a greater context, namely an integrated approach to deliver lasting value, efficacy, and efficiency.

The Tragedy of Twitter, a Symptom of a More Insidious Disease

I'm not calling it the 24th letter in the English alphabet. It's Twitter. When Elon Musk purchased the social media site in a billionaire's gambit, he fired more than half of its employees or they left. Personal and business accounts "randomly" lost followers. In 2022, Musk bought Twitter for $44 billion, declaring he'd restore "free speech." Chaos followed. Mass layoffs gutted trust and safety teams. Engineers who maintained the platform's infrastructure were fired. Hate speech surged as moderation crumbled. Musk rebranded Twitter as "X," erasing its legacy overnight. The blue bird was replaced by a stark black X, a tombstone for what it once was. His motives for the purchase continue to be examined through today.

Advertiser exodus was fast, as well as that of Twitter's top brass. At the time, Twitter was worth about $10 billion; he paid $44 billion. Brillant business move. But the astonishing premium may not have had anything to do with the purpose of the buy that was financed by powerful people from around the world. The premium had to be worth it to some powerful entities, and perhaps we are seeing that unfold now as many are calling out his censorship of a host of issues, but that's a rabbit hole for another day.

Marketing Mediocrity

I love what I do, but it can be a strange existence sometimes. My team and I educate clients as we plan and implement to ensure organizational learning is happening as we build campaigns and strategies. We approach marketing to help clients solve business problems. But as I've outlined, marketing right now is chaotic. Study after study shows people distrust marketers. A January 2022 Gallup Poll showed only 11 percent of people rated the advertising profession (advertising as an offshoot of marketing) as highly trusted, only two points above members of Congress who came in at 9 percent, and 3 percent higher than car salespeople who weighed in at 8 percent.[20]

And who can blame them? Never in the history of the world have people been the subject of more marketing, much of it bullshit. We're the most marketed people in the history of mankind. We live virtually on our mobile devices, and if we could, we'd live in them. For better or worse, our devices are the gateways to our hearts, minds, and wallets. Our screens bring us gossip, health, knowledge, news, groceries, rides, and riches, even sex. Our device vice is part and parcel of who we have become, an inextricable part of who we are. There's a visceral and deep emotional connection to our mobile devices, which is weird but true nonetheless. We get anxious when we're not with our phone. Devices are the singular source of immediate access to anything we desire and always accompanied by a hit of dopamine to make sure we come back again and soon. Our devices make us accessible to marketers, governments, and perhaps nefarious entities that we could not imagine. Nevertheless, the inextricable connection of devices to humans is a marketer's dream. With billions of people worldwide using smartphones and tablets, marketers can reach a vast audience anytime, anywhere. These devices provide a direct line to consumers through apps, social media, and mobile-optimized websites, enabling personalized and often real-time engagement. The data collected from mobile devices, such as location, browsing habits, and app usage, allows marketers to craft highly targeted campaigns, ensuring that advertisements reach the right audience with the right message. Just as important, the integration of mobile payment systems and e-commerce apps has streamlined the purchasing process, making it easier for consumers to act on marketing prompts faster than ever, and in some cases immediately, thereby increasing conversion rates and driving sales faster than ever.

But it's not only our devices where we are overwhelmed by marketing. We're subjected to rapid-fire messaging pollution from retargeting when visiting websites, robocalls, texts, and emails. And creative and messaging? Lots of it simply sucks. There's a sale every day on some websites, and we are reminded incessantly, if not badgered, to subscribe to email or SMS. "The pre-Black Friday Sale," "the Pre-Pre-Black Friday Sale," "The Return of Black Friday on a Tuesday," and so on. Every hospital wants you to know how unique they are by telling you they are "patient-centric," as if you can deliver healthcare by not being patient-centric. And while we're on the subject, why are not-for-profit hospitals sponsoring professional sports teams? As if, yeah, I'm in the middle of a Knicks-Celtics game and one day, if I ever need a hospital, I am going to remember that logo I saw in Madison Square Garden. I digress. Let's move to banking where every community bank is "the local community relationship bank." Marketing, including advertising, seems to suffer from delusional me-too-itis, because it's simpler and less controversial to copy competitors. Because if they're doing it, they must know something we don't. With all the marketing expertise out there, you'd think businesses can take more calculated risks, but from my little perch, the opposite is happening. It appears the more technological marketers have become, the less creative they're becoming and as a result, brands seem to be taking less risks, which may not be a bad thing. For the past several years in the U.S., "You" has taken over advertising. I'll name just a few: Burger King's "Have it Your Way," Buick's "So You," Toyota's "You wouldn't trust anyone to service your Toyota, would you?" and HBO's "You aren't just one you...." As if someone said, "People like themselves, talk about how great they are, link that to your brand, and voila!" And really, who can blame them? Or the ubiquitous email subject line "15% off, 25% off, 50% off!" Spare me! But why take risks with creative, even if it's well-research and executed, when brands could face a backlash on social media or when marketers can simply point to the competition and say, "They're doing it." Safety in messaging can be job security.

Pumping Out Ads, Content...Just Pump Them Out!

So yes, I'm in the camp of those who say the proliferation of marketing technologies has led us down the path of uninteresting marketing and digital waste. But it's not just uninteresting messaging. It's the absolute tyranny and ubiquity of platforms and channels, and the aggregation of human beings into two or three places like Facebook or Instagram, which are essentially the same place because they're owned by the same company. "Backlinks, can we do backlinks?" But they don't talk about website experience. What good is investing in backlinks or any modality that brings people to websites if the website experience sucks. "Google Ads..." Okay, do we have dedicated landing pages and auto-responses? Who is writing the ads? Are they compelling? Do we do A/B testing? So the nature of the default marketing discussion today is more and more about using platforms and less about *how* we will use them and if they are appropriate for what businesses are trying to achieve in the first place.

So, we live in unprecedented times, marked by an extraordinary level of connectedness through social media and digital apps, but also by extraordinary ignorance of how marketing works today; this issue is especially acute in middle markets and small business. Not only can we reach our family and friends around the world and see where they are and what they're doing, we can also invest and listen to music together. Consequently, we've granted social and digital platforms, and marketers and other actors, unprecedented access to our personal interests and habits, which is used to tailor our feeds to show us what they think we're interested in, based on what they know about us. They call this "personalized marketing." This personalized approach means that my social media feed can look dramatically different from my wife's, which looks dramatically different from our kids'.

Marketing today is in a frantic race to capture the most valuable commodity in the world: attention. The quest for potential minute-by-minute interaction with audiences is insatiable. Our scrolling habits, liking patterns, website visits, and sharing tendencies are a cornerstone of modern life. Marketers recognize the hypnotic power of these platforms and flock to them with unquestioning delusion and devotion, many times to the detriment of other marketing avenues, because digital marketing is "easy and tractable."

Analytics: The Great Hiding Place

While many businesses rely on social media influencers to promote their products and services, so too do social media and digital platforms in an almost perfect symbiotic relationship. Social media and digital marketing, powered by the same "thought leaders" in the Clickocracy, have ushered a golden era of perhaps intellectually lazy but frenzied autopilot marketing. Marketers have put their unquestionable trust and money in Google and Facebook because it's easy. They establish the parameters of their campaigns, set it, and wait for analytics to show their CEOs.

In 2022, I pitched a CMO of a global healthcare technology company. At the end of our meeting, he said, "Listen, my job is getting our content out there. Google and Facebook simplify things for our board and my CEO. I show them analytics; that's what they want to see because they see our competitors in the same space. It's what they like. You guys come in here and show them where and how dollars could be spent better; I can't have that. It makes me and my people look bad." While disappointed, I wasn't surprised because it wasn't the first time I've had that conversation. Self-preservation and waste win out in these situations, but the real winners are the platforms, and the loser is this guy's company, but they don't know that. So, he'll continue to pay Google and Facebook to produce the analytics he needs to pacify his board so he can keep his job. Ignorance is safe, and profitable for some.

Here's a more recent example. For about seven years, we worked with one of the world's largest distributors of healthcare products. It's predominately a sales organization, and in that type of business, marketing usually plays second fiddle. Part of our engagement was to help bridge the gap between sales and marketing, while helping the company move with more agility in the marketplace. As part of an organizational shift, two salespeople were put in charge of our marketing portfolio with the intent of integrating sales and marketing. As sales pros, both were digital marketing enthusiasts. One of them, let's call him John, had been promoted to lead the marketing enterprise of the business unit. The other, we'll call him Steve, was responsible for sales execution on leads delivered by John.

The company ended our engagement, deciding to replace us with a "digital marketing company" at lower costs. Through today, we still have a great relationship with the company and both John and Steve. After they transitioned the account to the new digital marketing company, John would call me occasionally, enthused by the number of leads he's getting from the new relationship whose campaigns are "amazing." "Our traffic is amazing now! And we're getting leads like never before!" he'd swoon. Though, when I talked with Steve about the state of the business, he'd say, "I've never wasted more time on useless leads. Yeah, we're getting more leads, but there's no quality. Crap leads...this is ridiculous. What are we paying those people for?" But since John is now being judged on traffic data analytics and the number of leads he acquires, he considers his performance to be "amazing" because he's delivering leads. He can rightly defend that to his boss. On the other hand, Steve, who was a distinguished sales professional, can't do anything with dead-end leads and is now considered a laggard in the company because he can't close (meaningless) leads. This fissure plays out repeatedly in our world, not just in between departments within companies, but also between companies and agencies.

Vanity metrics and performative marketing have exposed a delicious irony in corporate culture: the same organizations that preach "data-driven efficiency" often worship at the altar of *meaningless numbers*. Take Google—a company we'll politely call a "digital sleight-of-hand artist" for now. While its tools promise marketing clarity, they've masterfully engineered a hall of mirrors where businesses chase clicks like cats chasing laser pointers.

Google didn't simplify marketing; it turned it into a Rube Goldberg machine of ad spend. Through its programmatic platforms, it's achieved something truly awe-inspiring: convincing legions of CMOs that pouring money into algorithmic black boxes is "strategic." (Spoiler: Those boxes are less "black" and more "magic trick.") Studies, and bruised budgets, confirm the inefficiencies, yet the collective response is...meh. Why? Because admitting you've been outsmarted by a search engine is the corporate equivalent of yelling, "I paid $10,000 for this banana slicer ad to reach bots!"

But business leaders and many marketers and agencies aren't just passive victims. They're *willing accomplices*. By fetishizing vanity metrics (looking at you, "impressions") and outsourcing strategy to platforms' opaque algorithms, they've turned marketing into a wealth transfer scheme: from their balance sheets to Big Tech's offshore accounts. It's exhausting, isn't it? But that's their plan.

There's hope, though. It starts with asking Google the hard questions, like "Why does 'smart' bidding feel so...dumb?" or "Is 'reach' just a fancy word for 'spray and pray'?" Until then, we'll keep applauding the emperor's new analytics, because nothing says "efficiency" like paying for digital confetti. If marketing were a heist movie, Google would be the charming villain, and your CFO is the one holding the loot bag. Time to swap the rose-colored digital glasses for a magnifying glass. One more thought about Google here. It's not enough that their customer service team changes every three months so businesses who aren't spending millions a month never get to speak with a representative who understands their business to consult on how to best allocate advertising dollars on the platform. Instead, Google Ads' rotative account managers are there to encourage you to spend more to get more reach. This is a real voicemail left by a Google account manager on May 31, 2024:

Hey, this is [rep name], your Google Ads account manager for [client]. I've been trying to reach out to you since April 1st. Looking further into our account, I noticed that there's a major drop in the clicks and impressions that we've been receiving. And since I'd be your account manager till the end of this quarter, till June 31st, we are only left with one month of the complimentary consultation given by Google. So, I would want you to make complete use of it. So, give me a call back...and let me help you in, you know, fixing our account.

Google may say it wants to counsel businesses and agencies on better performance, but in my experience, Google's incentive is simple: to get businesses to spend more. How can an account manager get to know a business or a given market or product while on a three-month rotation? Utterly absurd. Google Ads account managers' only job is to get businesses to spend more money on Google. As for Facebook? If you manage to get someone on the phone, try to get them to give you the exact reach of your spend. Again, I am not saying these platforms don't work at all or businesses should not use them. Every business should, but they should do so with eyes wide open with the full recognition that an unknown portion of your ad dollars is going into a black hole of bots, fake sites, and fanatical algorithms that produce analytics and data.

Here's are a few rules for digital campaigns for clients:

- Ask better questions about analytics and don't fall in love with dashboards: What is the intent of the campaign? Branding, community building, awareness?
- Be clear about what you are measuring and why you need those numbers.
- Reaffirm that the entire digital marketing ecosystem is fraught with fraud but still a space for terrific opportunity.
- If there's an agency involved, know the incentives of your digital agency/partner.
- Ask about the true cost of digital advertising campaigns (net digital charges from the platform, plus commissions or markups).

- Fade your feelings. Your social media FOMO won't help you promote your business and only adds to the potential and real waste in the space.
- Social media's risks must be actively managed because businesses have already wasted billions on this autopilot mess.
- Do not mistake social media for digital marketing.
- Pre-determine how to leverage social platforms to ensure a consistent, on-brand experience for your audience.

Feeding the AdTech Beast That's Feasting on Us

I'm not a neuroscientist, but we have all come to recognize in some fashion that our brains don't know how to handle the onslaught of frequency and type of information we are subjected to. Luckily, Susan Greenfield, who is a neuroscientist, noted in a Neuromarketing Science and Business Association blog post, "As a neuroscientist I am very aware that the brain adapts to its environment. If you're placed in an environment that encourages a short attention span, which doesn't encourage empathy or interpersonal communication, which is partially addictive or compulsive...all these things will inevitably shape who you are. The digital world is an unprecedented one and it could be leaving an unprecedented mark on the brain."[21] Studies have shown that living on our devices can shorten attention spans, making it harder to sustain attention. The explosion of digital platforms and media fragmentation is impacting our ability to take in and process information. A study from Dartmouth found that the use of digital devices, such as tablets and laptops, for reading makes it more likely that we focus on concrete details rather than interpreting information more abstractly; this reduces our ability to think critically.[22]

There's a growing body of research on how digital media impacts our brains. In a 2018 piece in Harvard's *Science in the News*, Trevor Haynes said:

> Although not as intense as a hit of cocaine, positive social stimuli will similarly result in a release of dopamine, reinforcing whatever behavior preceded it. Cognitive neuroscientists have shown that rewarding social stimuli— laughing faces, positive recognition by our peers, messages from loved ones—activate the same dopaminergic

reward pathways. Smartphones have provided us with a virtually unlimited supply of social stimuli, both positive and negative. Every notification, whether it's a text message, a "like" on Instagram, or a Facebook notification, has the potential to be a positive social stimulus and dopamine influx.[23]

Businesses are hooked on the dopamine hits because humans run businesses. Validation for business is not just about selling their product; it's about likes, social proof. Big Tech and the AdTech industries have shaken the confidence of even the most rational marketing business leaders. This is psychological warfare. FOMO addiction is also real and preys on this addiction, because not being in the know is downright deadly in business. So, marketers and businesses, just like everyone else, have become addicted to Big Tech's dopamine hits. They are dependent on it. Like many addicts, businesses are left seeking the next high, but that's the cost of addiction. Like many addicts, they are in denial about whether this stuff works or not, whether their money is being spent responsibly and efficiently.

Marketing budgets sustain these digital beasts by feeding them with ad dollars. The absence of alternatives to Google, Facebook, and other major platforms, combined with the demise of alternative media, leaves us with the myth that digital media is the only game in town, and some perceive it as either free or much cheaper. The story marketers tell themselves and self-perpetuate is that digital media is more precise and can be tracked. But I submit that Big Tech has gotten marketers to abandon even entertaining other marketing vehicles. Businesses are submissively and willingly handing over dollars to an even more fragmented media ecosystem while competing for shorter attention spans. Shortened attention spans require more frequent messaging, more creativity to grab our attention. While we are just beginning to learn the impact of our digital lives on our human existence, the research on the subject is aplenty. Our perpetual connection to our mobile devices contributes to ADHD,[24] wear out the brain's pleasure centers,[25] impair social and emotional development,[26] and more. Every time we look at our mobile devices or any screen, we as consumers are perpetuating this problem.

"Fucking With the Magic"

The race for our attention is certain to become more intense. Marketers have been lulled into a digital marketing trance because, essentially, they've been indoctrinated and acculturated about how easy and cheap it is. We therefore also deduce that the attention of marketers has been compromised by the same technologies that plague consumers. An insidious and direct side effect of our manufactured marketing reality, aside from misspent dollars, is diluted and miscalculated marketing strategy. The auto-pilot digital approach is all too tempting. Disciplined and skeptical marketing professionals seemingly don't have a chance in this equation.

Some historical perspective is helpful to unravel how we got here. Our modern marketing cycle has only been around since 1998, when Google upended everything and changed the face of how we communicate and do business. In a heartbeat, Google pushed aside and displaced the brief market leadership of internet pioneers and innovators like AOL, Yahoo, and Excite. Facebook took it to an even more absurd level just 16 years later. In 2003, Viacom CEO Mel Karmazin visited Google, where Sergey Brinn and Larry Page showed him a new platform that allows advertisers to measure advertising effectiveness. Karmazin, whose business model relied on advertisers not knowing "what works and what doesn't. And that's a great model," immediately recognized Google's threat. He turned to Brinn and Page and blurted, "You're fucking with the magic." He was right. But Google actually fucked the magic and every media company on the planet, and a new force quickly arose transferring ad dollars from traditional media to digital. In his book *Googled*, Ken Auletta observed, "By May 2008, 220 million Americans had Internet access. While digital companies multiplied, between 2000 and 2007 traditional media companies lost 167,600 jobs—one out of every 6. The Internet ended the debate over whether content or distribution was king. The consumer was now king."[27]

There's clear a line of demarcation in marketing: BG, Before Google and AF, After Facebook. It was Facebook that transformed how we think about our world, neighbors, family, and friends. It spawned another level of AdTech marketing ecosystem at a scale and model that did not exist before. Whereas the consumer became the king with Google, Facebook, Twitter, and subsequently Instagram and TikTok, gave every person and business the power to be their own broadcasting entity, an opportunity to be their own brand. Businesses or individuals were now in a race to create content and get views and likes. Followers are key! The number of followers gave individuals and businesses power and influence. And so, the Facebook era gave birth to the social media influencer. At about the same time, Facebook and Google became the chief platforms promising to deliver advertising to the right person at the right time, allowing businesses to track their spend and media buy for pennies on the dollar. Digital marketing spurred unprecedented growth of digital agencies and in-house digital marketing teams across industries. The field is so hot, many universities got in on the action by offering certificates in social media, which is amusing and troubling because social media is simply a tool. There were no certificates in telephone sales when the telephone became pervasive. And while television advertising may be part of an advertising curriculum at colleges and universities, I am unable to find a program offering certificates in television advertising specifically. Universities are tempted by revenue associated with social media marketing, so I include them as a critical part of the Clickocracy. So now anyone who can set up a social media account and knows how to "create content" can sell themselves as a marketing expert or at the very least, a social media or digital marketing expert. From business to academia and beyond, the hype is real.

Another sector of the digital marketing game that's on fire right now is the creator economy. Insider Intelligence/e-Marketer estimates the creator economy to be worth about $100 billion. Brand sponsorships continue to be at the forefront as creators' number-one revenue stream in 2023, and creators continue to foster and push content while building their own networks.[28] Take a look at the approximate follower counts for the content creators mentioned (as of August 2024):

MrBeast (Jimmy Donaldson)
- **YouTube:** Over 200 million subscribers across his various channels, with his main channel being the most prominent.

PewDiePie (Felix Kjellberg)
- **YouTube:** Around 115 million subscribers on his main channel, making him one of the most subscribed individual creators on the platform.

Charli D'Amelio
- **TikTok:** Over 150 million followers, making her one of the most followed individuals on TikTok.
- **Instagram:** Around 50 million followers.

Emma Chamberlain
- **YouTube:** Approximately 12 million subscribers.
- **Instagram:** Around 16 million followers.
- **Podcast:** Her podcast "Anything Goes" has millions of downloads and a strong listener base.

The Try Guys
- **YouTube:** Around 8 million subscribers on their main channel.
- **Instagram:** Collectively, they have several million followers across their individual and group accounts.

No question, the turn to digital has created jobs and opportunities for individuals, businesses, entrepreneurs, and social movements (for good and ill). Digital marketing, while a powerful tool for reaching vast audiences, carries both impressive virtues and lamentable downsides. On the one hand, its ability to target specific demographics with precision is unmatched—consider how Facebook ads can home in on users based on their interests, behaviors, and even recent online activity, potentially leading to highly effective campaigns. Google Ads, with its ability to display search-based ads, allows businesses to capture potential customers at the exact moment they're looking for a product or service, often leading to higher conversion rates.

On the other hand, this very precision also underscores the troubling aspects of digital marketing, including digital advertising fraud. The relentless pursuit of data and the constant bombardment of tailored ads can feel invasive, eroding user privacy and contributing to an ever-growing sense of digital fatigue. Moreover, the same algorithms that drive success can also lead to echo chambers, where users are continually exposed to content that reinforces their existing beliefs, rather than broadening their horizons. As we marvel at the capabilities of digital marketing, it's worth remembering that these tools, when misused, can diminish the very human experiences they aim to enhance. In the next chapter, we'll explore Big Tech's stranglehold on marketing, the players, and tactics. Let's go!

3 Uber Fraud

If Uber lost $100 million on digital ads, do you stand a chance? In 2017, Uber uncovered a massive flaw in its digital advertising strategy: two-thirds of its $150 million ad budget, roughly $100 million, was being drained by fraudulent or ineffective digital placements. The revelation came amid public scrutiny over Uber ads appearing on Breitbart, a far-right platform known for extremist rhetoric, which clashed with the company's professed inclusive values. The double blow: wasted spend on bot-driven fraud and brand damage from controversial ad placements and exposed systemic vulnerabilities in digital advertising's opaque supply chain, sparking industry-wide debates about transparency, accountability, and the hidden costs of "growth at all costs."

Unknowingly to Uber's marketing leadership, its digital ads were sucking an epic $100 million of its $150 million ad budget. This underscored the idea that even the most seasoned, well-financed marketing organizations can fall prey to the intricacies of the AdTech industrial complex. After the investigation, Kevin Frisch, Uber's former head of performance, marketing, and consumer relations management, said, "We turned off two-thirds of spending. And basically, saw no change." What Kevin did was remove $100 million from his ad spend, and saw no difference in performance, defined as "app installs," at the time. Kevin's advice? "You should start by assuming that half of what's on the display channels is fraud."[29]

Businesses shout from the rooftops about managing efficiently, yet in fact we live in a more complicated, paradoxical world. Like many things in our earthly existence, multiple truths can live comfortably side by side. People can say they manage by data when, in fact, they don't or don't know how. The same people who don't manage by data say they use analytics to make decisions when they know or are ignorant of the fact those analytics mean nothing. It's a wild world. Right now, the prevailing wisdom driven by Clickocrats tells us every business is a technology business, every business is a content producer, and Google search is the center of the universe. The truth is maybe for some, not for others. Successful businesses understand the nuances of when and how to deploy anything digital, from ads to organic content. That nuance can free them from being blind slaves to marketing technologies.

Consuming Content

For many businesses, content marketing has evolved into a multi-faceted engine for growth, blending traditional digital foundations with dynamic social strategies. While some companies thrive with streamlined digital presences, such as service guides and websites packed with value-driven blogs, others amplify their reach through social media. A home improvement contractor, for instance, might dominate local search results with a polished site and glowing reviews, while also leveraging Instagram Reels to showcase renovation transformations or TikTok tutorials on DIY trends. Similarly, B2B enterprises often marry LinkedIn thought leadership articles with YouTube explainer videos and email nurture campaigns, creating a content web that educates decision-makers at every touchpoint. The key lies in aligning tactics to audience behavior: not every business needs a viral Twitter thread or Pinterest mood board, but those that strategically layer social storytelling, video demos, or podcast partnerships atop core digital assets often unlock disproportionate visibility in an over-saturated market.

According to Search Engine Land's interpretation of Google's recent leaked internal documents about its search algos, "If you want to rank well, you need to keep creating great content and user experience."[30] But what the hell does that mean? Creating content, let alone great content, can be rewarding, but it's usually time-consuming, expensive, and risky, especially for the middle market and small businesses. Not to mention, content produced for search can be different than for social. For example, companies like Morgan Stanley or GE's business models don't require the same content marketing strategies as Coca-Cola or Nike. Morgan Stanley's brand and storytelling on social takes a different form and tone than it does in its search strategies. So, different businesses require different ways of producing content to engage customers on search and social. While Coca-Cola's marketing success over the years can be credited to its long-standing omnichannel strategy, the rise of digital media gave the company an opportunity to speak and directly engage its customers. Coke's success is not tied to search but it's betting that its future is. Coke continues to find success, growing its influence through digital entertainment. In 2008, the company launched Coke Studios in Pakistan, a music platform that engages its global stage. Coke Studios' YouTube Channel is always on and now has over 14 million subscribers as I type. One of its songs, *Pasoori* by Ali Sethi and Shae Gill, has an astonishing 572 million views. This is on top of everything else Coke does on the marketing side to make Coke the global brand juggernaut.

Digital marketing in virtually every sector has become both essential and gamified. Surgeons don't just do surgery; they have podcasts. They take videos while performing surgeries and post them on social media shortly after. Sometimes, they live stream from the OR. These surgeons, like the pizza shop or hardware store, must feed the insatiable beast of social media. Social media has turned many businesses and professionals into performers, dancing to the tune of digital platforms for their brand to stay ahead of their perceived competition, satisfying both their ego and perceived impact on their business. There's little room for doubt that digital marketing is the chief culprit of unprecedented ad dollar fraud, business process inefficiencies, and misplaced investment. Just on the advertising side alone, studies have shown programmatic digital advertising is responsible for a staggering $80 billion to $120 billion in fraud.

Let's examine a few cases where companies took a more critical look at their digital strategies. Some of these may surprise you. Take, for example, Simple Modern, whose co-founder posted a Twitter thread for the ages about his experience with Amazon Ads. Simple Modern had spent $10 million on Amazon Ads and for a month they decided to spend $0. There was no issue with their Amazon Ads; they worked. The company decided to challenge its own assumptions and analytics and quickly found out their Amazon Ads didn't work as well as they thought. The company had a history of spending 8 percent of revenue on advertising, which bought top placement on Amazon and intuitively seemed like it was producing results. Simple Modern began to notice they were paying for organic purchases with ads, meaning customers who found them organically or were going to purchase anyway were clicking on the ads to buy. A total waste. So, their solution was to drop their brand keyword "Simple Modern." Simple Modern's examination of its digital ad spend and efficacy is rare actually, though a terrific case of how one company improved digital marketing performance and saved money by challenging its own assumptions.

As much as time, energy, and money is focused on search marketing, social media continues to be the darling of digital marketers everywhere. "What are we doing on social? Insta Reels or Facebook? What about TikTok?" Time and again, when we ask them to dig into social's organic analytics, they usually deflect by talking about content production. Based on my experience with businesses of all sizes across industries and at various stages of their lifecycle social media, organic and paid ads are by far the most popular and the least understood. Here are a few mindboggling stats from Rival IQ that illustrate the gravity of the social media problem. In its 2023 Social Media Industry Benchmark Report, Rival IQ found the median engagement for organic posts on Facebook by followers of businesses across sectors is .06 percent.[31] Point Zero Six. I'm no math whiz, but that doesn't seem very good. In fact, "pitiful" would be a nice way to put it. Let's break that down a bit. It means that if you had 1,000 relevant people, true believers in your brand, on your business Facebook, and you posted organically, .6 people actually engaged in the post. That's a little more than half a person. That's the average. Meaning for some industries, like healthcare, it's .03 percent. Anyone with access to oxygen and a relatively developed frontal lobe knows this doesn't make any sense, yet businesses remain willfully ignorant, overlook these realities and march on because "everybody is doing it." It's fair to say that businesses and brands are awash with data, but the question remains, what are we doing with that data? Businesses have demonstrated over and over that changing their behavior is difficult, even in the face of data. Why? One of the reasons is that changing strategies, let alone admitting something isn't working, is both painful and embarrassing. No one likes admitting that the strategies they are responsible for were

> **"Facebook's algorithms prioritize divisive content to maximize engagement, drowning out legitimate businesses in a sea of misinformation and clickbait."**
>
> —Frances Haugen, Facebook whistleblower, in testimony to U.S. Congress (October 2021)

ineffective. No one wants their work examined. It's the very essence of self-preservation and I get that. It's a dangerous game depending on where one sits in their organization.

Social media is a *Faustian bargain*. Today, every scroll, like, and share feeds a parasitic ecosystem where brands have unwittingly become digital sharecroppers, toiling on platforms that profit not just from their ad dollars, but from their labor. Agencies and marketing teams now function as content mills, churning out posts to appease algorithmic overlords; modern-day serfs paying rent with mind-numbing human "creativity," data, and attention. The cost is the tax I mentioned earlier, and worth repeating: a toxic cycle where businesses bleed budgets and sanity, shackled to platforms that sell their audiences back to them as ads, while harvesting user data for third-party brokers.

As I mentioned earlier, the gravest threat isn't financial; it's the surrender of imagination. Like moths to a flame, marketers now chase digital validation, their creativity and business sense hollowed out by the dopamine chase of likes and shares. This isn't just a distraction; it's business and cultural surrender. The feed's tyranny has narrowed vision to a flickering screen, where strategies atrophy and originality starves. Breaking free isn't mere courage, it's *war*—a war against complacency, against the seductive lie that "engagement" equals impact, and for every dollar spent to promote a business. Victory demands ruthless prioritization: not retreat, but *revolution*. Big Tech knows this, that's why they're armed to the teeth in every major capital. CMOs must audit platforms like shrewd negotiators.

Reclaim stolen attention. Redirect resources to channels where brands build legacies, not just metrics, where storytelling isn't throttled by an algorithm's whims. This rebellion isn't anti-technology; it's pro-business and pro–common sense. It's choosing to be architects of meaning, not sharecroppers on digital plantations. The future doesn't favor those who kneel. It belongs to those who wield platforms as tools, not temples.

In his incendiary book *AdScam*, Bob Hoffman, one of the marketing and Big Tech industries' fiercest critic and self-proclaimed "Ad Contrarian," pulls back the curtain on the grotesque underbelly of digital advertising and reveals how digital marketing fraudsters are stealing billions. With razor-sharp insight, he exposes AdTech's hypnotic grip on marketers and unflinchingly confronts the elephant in the room: ad fraud is an open secret no one wants to talk about.

Programmatic advertising, Hoffman argues, is the "greatest scam in marketing history." "When you buy a fake Rolex," he writes, "the fraudster at least has to produce a watch. But when you buy ads on a fake website, they don't even have to build one."

The numbers are staggering. According to Advertising Age and Spider Labs, 20 percent of global online ad budgets, "roughly $70 billion in 2022 alone, are siphoned off by fraudsters." That's not inefficiency. That's industrial-scale theft, enabled by an industry too dazzled by its own hype to stop it. The question isn't whether marketers are being robbed; it's how long they'll keep pretending it isn't happening.

AdTech companies, along with Big Tech (Google, Facebook, Apple, Twitter, Microsoft, etc.), have created a black box designed to suck in ad dollars and spit out analytics, which makes people feel better about how they spend because they can "see" where and how their budget is being deployed. You'll know exactly what you're putting in but never really know what you're getting out of it. We've known for a while that programmatic ad dollars aren't efficiently spent nor deployed responsibly and honestly by Big Tech. Thankfully the veil is slowly being lifted. Advocates and marketing experts like Bob Hoffman, Nadini Jammi, and Dr. Augustine Fou have done much research in the field and are leading voices that should be amplified. Not only are they voices of reason backed by years of research and experience, but their approach also makes business sense. I encourage you to follow their work to get a deeper understanding of the gravity of the problems facing the marketing industry and what you can do about it, because the consequences of feeding Big Tech go far beyond marketing. These folks aren't household names; you won't see their posts or quotes shared nearly as often as the marketing geniuses yelling at you from the back of the cab or on YouTube pre-roll ads. We live in a world where confident, sometimes lucky, often incompetent voices are elevated, simply because of their ability to perform over the thoughtful and contemplative. More than ever, our world is proving to value popularity or entertainment more than substance. Yet, despite business's bravado about discipline anchored in efficiency and driven by data, it really isn't. The reality is, if businesses are run by humans, they'll behave just as we humans do: illogically and irrationally.

Data offers a sense of certainty, objectivity, and (sometimes false) security in an otherwise complex and unpredictable field. Click-through rates or conversion rates can seem like reliable guides for decision-makers. However, like the example I shared earlier of my interaction with the CMO of a large healthcare company, reliance on data can be a dangerous adventure. Without proper context or critical analysis, reliance on data can lead to misinformed strategies or perhaps an exercise in pacification and compliance. For example, focusing solely on high-traffic website numbers might obscure the fact that much of that traffic is not converted because a good chunk of the traffic is bot driven, not human. So, will anyone ask if the traffic is human or bots? Another downside of an overemphasis on data is the throttling of creativity and innovation, reducing marketing efforts to a series of numbers, a spreadsheet item. Rather, give teams opportunities to explore and pursue more meaningful, human-centered strategies, while at the same time including digital in their mix. Balancing data with qualitative insights, like customer feedback and market trends, can be crucial to fostering creativity for marketers and their teams. They should also develop a strong understanding of the context behind the data, ensuring that they interpret it correctly and use it to inform, not dictate, strategic decisions. Training and experience in the nuances of both data interpretation and creative marketing, not just in producing reports, are essential to avoid the pitfalls of data-only dependency.

How about Chick-fil-A's more recent decision to cut back on their digital advertising spend. Instead of relying heavily on paid digital ads,

Chick-fil-A shifted its focus to community-based marketing and improving the customer experience in their restaurants. They invested in employee training, customer service, and in-store technology improvements, which led to a better overall customer experience. This strategy paid off, as the company continued to see growth in sales and brand loyalty, despite spending less on digital ads. Diageo, the global beverage giant behind brands like Johnnie Walker and Guinness, reduced its digital ad spend as part of a broader strategy to improve its return on investment (ROI). The company realized that a significant portion of its digital ads were not effectively reaching its target audience. By cutting back on these inefficient spends, Diageo redirected its budget towards more traditional and experiential marketing strategies, such as events and in-person experiences, which aligned better with its brand identity. This shift not only saved money but also strengthened customer engagement and brand perception.

There are many more cases like this that don't get enough attention in the business press and are dually ignored by the so-called marketing influencers pontificating on stage or live streaming from a jog. I will leave with you one more from one of the world's largest marketers, Procter & Gamble. In 2017, P&G decided to slash its digital advertising budget by $200 million. This decision was based on concerns about the effectiveness of their digital ad spend, especially given the issues of ad fraud, poor targeting, and ads being placed next to inappropriate content. Despite cutting back on digital ads, P&G reported that their brand visibility did not suffer; in fact, they saw improved reach and engagement. The company attributed this to a more strategic approach to ad placements, focusing on quality over quantity. P&G's experience demonstrates that reducing digital spend, when combined with smarter, more targeted marketing strategies, can actually enhance overall effectiveness and ROI.[32]

Here's the crazy thing: most people don't know about Uber's colossal fraud case, nor P&G's shift on digital. Why isn't the business media, which extols efficiency up and down, in a frenzy to warn businesses about this? Why aren't they celebrating P&G's decision and the people who made those moves? Why aren't the people who lament government's inefficiencies sounding the alarm or issuing white papers on digital fraud or the many examples of marketing waste outlined in these pages?

Marketing Is Human

Someone much wiser than me once said, "People shop with their brains but buy with their hearts." Naturally, that's why you see emotional appeals in advertising. Remember Pet Rock? What was the emotion around that phenomenon? What about cigarettes and sugary drinks? Investing legend and Warren Buffet's partner Charlie Munger once said, "How could economics not be behavioral? If it isn't behavioral, what the hell is it?" So, what the hell is marketing if it isn't behavioral? We can't discuss marketing without establishing its foundation in human or consumer behavior and behavioral economics, which is the answer to the question of what motivates people to buy. Behavioral economics should be part of every university's marketing curriculum and embedded in the DNA of marketers because customer motivation, often not rational, is at the heart of preference and buying decisions.

Marketing is simple. Consumer habits and tastes, across age, income, and other variables, can be manufactured and shaped. That sounds blasphemous but think diamonds for engagements and weddings, Black Friday madness, and Americans learning a new language to order coffee at Starbucks in venti, grande, and trenta sizes. Those were manufactured. So, marketing is behavior modification or behavior reinforcement. We don't like to admit it, but much of what we think has been our freedom to choose a product, lifestyle, or even political positions, has been shaped or directly manufactured through psychological manipulation and keen understanding of human behavior.

Let's explore one example of how Big Tobacco made it more culturally acceptable for women to smoke in public in order to sell more cigarettes. In the late 1920s, smoking was taboo for women; they smoked mostly indoors. Big Tobacco was looking for a way for them to smoke outside because it was free advertising and a way to significantly sell more cigarettes. They tapped Edward Bernays, considered the father of public relations, who rode the coattails of the women's liberation movement to successfully sell cigarettes. In 1929, he organized a group of women to march in New York City's Easter parade, holding cigarettes, which were referred to as "torches of freedom." As a 2008 article in the *New York Times* put it, quoting Bernay's biography by Larry Tye:

Ten young women turned out, marching down Fifth Avenue with their lighted "torches of freedom," and the newspapers loved it. Two-column pictures showed elegant ladies, with floppy hats and fur-trimmed coats, cigarettes held self-consciously by their sides, as they paraded down the wide boulevard. Dispatches ran the next day, on page one, in papers from Fremont, Nebraska, to Portland, Oregon, to Albuquerque, New Mexico.

The *New York Times* published an article the next day on the Easter Parade, with headline saying in part, "Group of Girls Puff at Cigarettes as a Gesture of 'Freedom[.]'"

"Within a year, it became acceptable for woman to smoke outside," Dr. Jackler said. The cigarettes became known as "torches of freedom."[33]

Let's explore the uniquely American phenomenon of pharmaceutical advertising. Pharmaceutical drug marketing often employs strategies that encourage consumers to identify with specific health conditions, sometimes leading them to believe they may have an illness or disorder that requires treatment, even if their symptoms are minimal or non-existent. These multi-million-dollar marketing campaigns often emphasize vague symptoms that many people experience at some point, such as fatigue, mild anxiety, or occasional discomfort, and suggest that these could be signs of a more serious condition requiring pharmaceutical intervention. By promoting awareness of these symptoms that we all feel at one point or another in our lives, and pointing to the availability of treatments, drug companies create a demand among people who may not genuinely need them. Studies have shown pharmaceutical advertising can lead to overdiagnosis and overtreatment, where individuals are prescribed medications for conditions that are not clinically significant, ultimately contributing to increased healthcare costs and potential side effects from unnecessary drug use.

One notable example is the marketing of drugs for conditions like "generalized anxiety disorder," "low testosterone," or men over 40 feeling tired. Men over 40 feeling tired? No way, that doesn't happen to anyone I know! Like "men over 40 feeling tired," some of these symptoms can be common and nonspecific, leading many to seek medical help for what might be normal variations in mood or aging. This continues to raise ethical concerns about the role of pharmaceutical companies in shaping public perceptions of health and illness. But Big Pharma is appealing to the growing demographic of older Americans. The industry is savvy. You see, "The number of Americans ages 65 and older is projected to increase from 58 million in 2022 to 82 million by 2050 (a 47% increase), and the 65-and-older age group's share of the total population is projected to rise from 17% to 23%," according to a study by the Population Reference Bureau in January 2024.[34] And if we take the lazy approach and say men represent 50 percent of those numbers, it's quite an opportunity for Big Pharma, isn't it? So, if shaping consumer behavior, tastes, and preferences is at the root of marketing, what fundamental questions can we ask to best position our marketing strategies? While they seem rudimentary, here's where I start:

1. A comprehensive review of the most basic: product, price, place, and promotion (the 4 Ps).
2. Where do customers, users, fans, and buyers come from?
3. What are the triggers connected to the specific product or category that lead consumers to buy or shun your product, service, or idea?
4. What, if any, are the cultural or social forces or connections we can make to your product, service, or idea?
5. How can we invent scenarios and creative that connect buyers to your products, ideas, and services? (If that sounds like propaganda to you...bingo!)

These foundational questions are the pillars of how we position campaigns. From here, we can move to customer motivation and understand buying behaviors, budgets, platforms, and so on. It's strange for conventional economics to toe the strict line of supply, demand, and price when we all live a vastly different experience. As we're pondering all these questions, it's also helpful to think about the following:

- Why do we overpay for Air Jordans?
- Why buy a Mercedes when a Chevy gets the same exact job done for much less?
- Why do people respond better to "buy one get one free" better than "buy two get 50 percent off"?

- Why do people continue to invest in a stock when it continues to decline, even if it means risking more losses?

- Why do people believe former Speaker of the House of Representatives Newt Gingrich is a harbinger of conservative values when he's lived a life of infidelity, cheated on his wife while she was on her death bed, and was divorced 3 times? (If you're a Republican and are offended by this for some reason, even though it's the truth, insert your favorite Democrat who's successfully lied to the public and continues to thrive.)

- Why do people spend $4 on coffee every day when they could make it at home for pennies?

- Why do people spend $7 on a hotdog at a baseball game but think paying $6 for a pack of 12 at the supermarket is too much?

Customers are neither rational nor logical, so I encourage our clients to think along that realm. Nine out of 10 times, that is an awkward and uncomfortable conversation. The comfort zone is a familiar place where their products and competitors are neatly organized and there's often a linear progression from what the customer wants and their product or service. "Logic is conventional and there's a price to be paid for being conventional," quipped Rory Southerland in his book, *Alchemy*. As the vice chairman for Ogilvy, he went on to establish a department within the firm that finds counterintuitive solutions to problems, because humans are driven by something other than rational economic theory. Despite the dogmatic digital herd mentality from the Clickocracy, we have learned that markets aren't rational or efficient because people aren't rational.

Digital dopamine aside, paying closer attention to customer motivation should be at the top of every marketer's list, working to solve the problem backwards from customer motivation back to the product or service. The old saying, "People shop with their brains but buy with their hearts" underscores the primal role emotion plays in purchasing decisions. When a customer needs a wasp repellent because they just saw a hive by the front door and rushes to a hardware store, their choice of repellent is not just transactional; it's a visceral response to fear, urgency, and the instinct to protect themselves or their family. Here, psychology and product placement collide to shape the outcome. So buyer motivation and psychology come into play.

In this case, the customer's decision is driven by emotional urgency, fear of attack, or the growing hive, and "practical necessity" is immediate relief. In this heightened state, the customer defaults to cognitive short-cuts: familiarity, convenience, and visual salience. A recognized brand offers perceived reliability, reducing risk in a stressful moment. Price matters, but not as a primary factor. When emotions run high, speed of decision-making often trumps frugality. Packaging color or design can subconsciously signal efficacy (e.g., bold red for "danger" or green for "natural safety"), while shelf placement determines visibility.

Contributing to the customer's calculus and decision is product place-ment. The three brands on the shelf face an unequal battle. The eye-level product gains an automatic advantage. Eighty percent of purchases are driven by ease of access, as stressed customers rarely bend or reach. The "Coca-Cola Rule" (eye-level placement drives sales) and studies by orga-nizations like POPAI (Point of Purchase Advertising International) found that 70–80 percent of purchase decisions are made in-store, heavily influ-enced by visibility and accessibility. A 1995 Coca-Cola study famously claimed that moving products to eye level increased sales by 20–30 per-cent, reinforcing the idea that placement drives decisions. A brightly col-ored package disrupts the visual field, while a premium price might para-doxically signal "quality" in a split-second judgment. However, if a brand has preemptively built trust through ads or word-of-mouth, it becomes the mental default, bypassing deliberation entirely. Which one of these prod-ucts gets plucked off the shelves?

Ultimately, the customer grabs the repellent that "feels" right in the moment, a blend of instinct, accessibility, and subconscious brand imprint-ing. For marketers, winning that critical seconds-long battle hinges on understanding not just the brain, but the heartbeat of the decision.

Let's examine Apple customers' undying devotion and love affair with the company. Apple users feel things about the brand, don't they? Apple achieves this by deploying several key psychological principles to cultivate and maintain the strong connection between its products and consum-ers. The brand has done a masterful job in connecting its products into their consumers' personal self-expression, even identity. Apple's aesthetic design, look and feel of its website and TV commercials, innovative fea-tures, and high cost allow users to feel that owning an Apple product says something about who they are personally, whether that's being creative, tech-savvy, or sophisticated. To a lesser extent, but no less important, Apple has cultivated a "tribe" mentality, giving people a sense of belonging to the "Apple community." This can make switching to Android feel like leaving a personal or group identity behind, and therefore difficult, if not physically painful. Other factors that contribute to the psychological hold Apple has on customers include Apple's UX, which is designed to become part of daily routines, forming habits. The more people use Apple products, the more automatic it becomes, reinforcing their reliance on the brand, and the more painful it becomes to leave the product.

A Word, or Two, About B2B Marketing

Let's talk about a segment that doesn't' get much love, the B2B space. B2B marketing is full of features and technical specs. No one is ever fired for producing less copy in a sell sheet or presentation, and emotional levers are rarely used. But if you think about it, buyers and sellers in the B2B space are people and they are subject to branding and emotive messaging. Right before COVID, we engaged a Michigan-based company in the healthcare training space. The CEO reached out because he wanted to grow through social media, mainly LinkedIn. It makes sense to think that his buyers are active on the leading business social platform and therefore he thought focusing there would be a safe place to tell his company's story. Yet, the company's training modules were largely offline at the time, and training was in person for the most part. So, we worked with them through digital transformation first, digitizing their training and creating an online marketplace, an app, and an ecommerce site for their non-training products. You certainly could not scale that type of business without digital transformation, and what good is investing in marketing to drive the brand and leads if we can't deliver an excellent product and customer experience? Second, we quickly affirmed that for the foreseeable future, the primary customer was their distributor network, so we suggested tabling LinkedIn to focus digital strategies on increased webinar partnerships with distributors and partners with much larger customers bases that can put them in front of potential customers, like associations, distributors, and industry partners. We also hypothesized that while customers may like or engage with us on their feed, which is good for brand awareness, the pitch and path to purchase was a bit more complicated. With limited resources, we needed to capture our customers' attention and create a walled garden where our message was the only message. Dealing with distributors provided a built-in market and relevant customers that we can acquire at much lower costs than direct to customer marketing at that time. We also knew distributors and other partners were looking for relevant content to engage mutual customers, and our client's content was exceptional. We decided to put the CEO in front of these audiences because he's well-liked and respected in the industry. His stature and nurturing demeaner on full display, we knew he would draw audiences, and he would both educate them and alleviate the fears of the customer for not training their people, which is an essential part of the sell. We averaged about 70 webinars per year for each of the past four years. Once a webinar was over, sales came in immediately after and if not, partners would share the list of attendees, which allowed us to be included in a drip email marketing campaign. The business grew steadily while their LinkedIn following remained largely flat, around 350 followers. We used LinkedIn to push messaging, humble-brag about webinars, and share partner announcements, but our laser focus was on executing webinars by showcasing the likeability and expertise of the CEO. By consistently showcasing the CEO's considerable people skills, through the distribution network that provides captive customers and social proof at the same time, we were able to deliver conversions almost immediately after webinars and through drip emails campaigns going forward. In speaking with the CEO today, he looks back amused at the thought of trying to grow the business on LinkedIn.

Other Behavioral Consideration

Let's delve into how customer behavior puts us in the right direction to develop and distribute a brand efficiently. We start with these five questions:

1. **Customer motivation.** Why would or should consumers buy your stuff? Costs less? Cool brand? New trends? Convenience? Makes me feel better about myself? A combination or all of these?

2. **Customer perception cultivation.** How people perceive your product, service, or brand greatly impacts their buying decision. What do they need to hear, see, and feel? What's the story? What does creative look like? What platforms do you use, on and offline, the tone and cadence of your message? These and more come together to shape consumer perception and create an impression or imprint on your customers.

3. **Feelings.** Your brand should create an emotional response to ensure you connect with your customers on a deeper level that inspires them to buy your stuff. What are those feelings?

4. **Social proof.** Way before Google Reviews and Yelp, there was word of mouth. It's still there and it's still one of the most potent marketing tools; ignore it at your peril. Whether online reviews or offline discussions, people have a natural need to validate their own decisions. "Oh, other people think this so it must be good (or bad)." Make sure social proof is part of your planning, and ensure you gather customer reviews and testimonials to show customers many others have chosen to buy.

5. **Campaign distribution.** Where and how can we focus the brand or campaign message with overwhelming force and frequency?

4 The Marketing Mindset

Marketing pros must subscribe to a mindset or a philosophy if they're going to consistently play the game well; and they must also follow a process connected to that philosophy. The game and your opponents may be different each time you play, but principles should not change. Our core philosophy drives every engagement, and we start with a conversation where we outline these principles with clients:

- The client is not always right. We are not always right. We work together. Social media is a thing, but not the main thing. Make sure the conversation is focused on client goals first.
- Zero hype. If there's data, then present it and we will interpret to the best of our abilities. If the data is bullshit, let's call that. If there's no data, let's go with experience fully knowing that we may fail and plan on getting back on the horse quickly.
- Ensure the marketing brief is translated into a solid plan with wiggle room.

- Execute on creative.
- Execute on rollout.
- Review and adjust where appropriate.

Marketing Is Not a Democracy

We firmly believe marketing is not an exercise in democracy. Remember what happened with our bank earlier? We live in the real world, meaning we believe not everyone is qualified to comment on marketing and not all opinions bear equal weight. Living in the real world recognizes that outstanding results are possible but also failure is likely. One day your campaigns are running high, the next they're completely dry; the following day, month, quarter you're roaring again.

H2 Oh! Humbling and Hard!

Marketing is plagued by many things right now, but nothing stifles marketing professionals more than short-termism and group think. Whether created by marketing pros themselves or their superiors, short-termism and "consensus" dominates business thinking and today's dizzying marketing landscape. As a result, it's fairly common for marketing pros to get hammered from many places in their organization about today's performance. That's why it's important to build a space and mindset for resiliency. For me, that mindset starts with humility.

A 2021 Deloitte Study found only 26 percent of CEOs trust their CMO.[35] Certainly in my experience, the C-Suite harbors much skepticism of marketing, sometimes rightfully so. A May 2022 study by Spencer Stuart, the search advisory firm, found the average tenure of a Chief Marketing Office is about 40 months.[36] The pressure on CMOs to produce results, regardless of the lifecycle of the business or product, is palpable. At the heart of all of this, of course, is businesses' obsession and, many times, delusion with endless economic expansion.

The outcomes of both studies are troubling but reflective of the larger reality in the world in which we live. A dangerous blend of unrealistic growth expectations, tension over budgets, vanity analytics, FOMO marketing, and civilians with Facebook accounts masquerading as marketing professionals come together to create a toxic cocktail for marketers. Expectations of marketers are unrealistically through the roof right now. Experienced CMOs, brand managers, and marketing pros do not participate in any of this nonsense, of course, but are nonetheless affected by it. Elite marketers know that they are not running a stock trading station and understand how to play the marketing game to achieve results and manage internal expectations.

Enter humility. I know it's not part of our brash business. Give me your 30-second elevator pitch bullshit playbook these days. But if you're in marketing, humility can be your superpower. Want to be trusted? Humility can help bridge the trust gap between marketers and the C-suite because executive teams and business owners need to understand exactly what you do, how you do it, and what it means to the performance of the overall business. They too are subjected to marketing propaganda and noise, so it's incumbent on you to engage them constructively. Humility then opens the door to more honest, perhaps less contentious conversations with colleagues, and becomes an indispensable tool to allow your organization to trust marketing's work.

Too many marketers don't know how or are unwilling to say, "I don't know why that campaign didn't work." You're probably thinking there's no way I'm ever admitting to my boss that I don't know something because you're putting your expertise in question, and who wants to do that? But before we get to the "I don't know why" conversation, let's talk about how you get to humility more comfortably and ensure your organization perceives and understands it as sincere and coming from a position of strength rather than a weakness.

The road to a more honest "I don't know" conversation is rooted in deeper relationships, practice, preparation, and game-planning your campaign strategies. Sometimes campaigns work, and other times they don't. Sometimes they work well, sometimes they deliver mediocre results, other times the results are terrible. That is not my opinion; that is a simple fact every business needs to face. And sometimes, we don't know why it went one way or the other; it's just what happens. The sooner your boss and teams come to terms with this law of marketing gravity, the better all of you become at the game and the more critical you'll become of your own marketing processes. Like shooting free throws, it takes repetition. The

> **"Marketing is like threading a needle. You have to balance global appeal with local relevance, and that's incredibly hard to scale."**
>
> —Indra Nooyi (Former CEO, PepsiCo) *Harvard Business Review* interview (2019)

more you do it, the better you'll become and the more your team will trust you. I am assuming competence and good work here, because if people suck at marketing, then this humility won't save them.

Internal marketing leaders should lean into their company's culture and expectations. What type of realistic marketing strategies can you develop with your resources and talent? Is the culture open or limiting? The same questions apply to agencies working with clients. Situational awareness also means recognizing your CEO may be reading marketing stuff and comparing notes with colleagues. The proliferation of business media, blogs, email newsletters, and the speed and frequency in which they reach their target certainly isn't conducive to constructive, well-thought-out conversations. Many of these are read out of context. They're quick and dirty. You probably get the same stuff in your email that I do. The non-stop marketing newsletters beat the drums of successful campaigns. Even when a campaign is banal at best, they'll tell you it rocks. But banal "is" content, and if it's on an email platform, it must be good, right?

Successful campaigns, the majority anecdotal and not replicable, headline every email newsletter or LinkedIn post showcasing the one campaign that got a million social media impressions in 48 hours. The problem is, in my experience, the reader is often excited and anesthetized by the sugar high of the campaign, which disables the part of the brain that asks critical questions, such as "Can we actually replicate this strategy for our business?" So, the reader's expectations become, however erroneous, that they can run similar campaigns because if "They can do it, so can we." But it's not just the hype that makes it to your inbox—marketing BS is everywhere! I've never been to a conference where the person on stage didn't produce some ridiculous year-over-year growth number. Like some magical marketing fantasy lands, conference stages are full of people whose campaigns never fail nor sputter. They paint a world where there's nothing to learn from failure, only success. It's as predictable as a 30-minute American sitcom. I find it curious and infuriating that these marketing "thought leaders," who speak with the unbridled confidence of caffeinated Greek gods, usually tell you what to do, but never seem to convey how to do it. Why? Because dollars to donuts, they don't know and they can't replicate their own campaign success if their life depended on it. Indeed, if they experienced success, they'll be hard-pressed to replicate it. These people are excellent storytellers, and storytelling rules the day in this field. Know this fundamental truth: marketing failure or success could be a result of impeccable planning, randomness, hard luck, or great timing. Marketing is governed and complicated by the laws of personal motivation at the time and place in which they live, and macroeconomics that work at the same time. So we must understand that marketing is ripe with failure; it's part of the job. If failing fast is a steadfast business principle, it should be pinned on the wall of every marketer's office. Just like turnovers in a basketball game, marketers need to get back and play defense, get the ball back and move on to the next play. So embrace those failures when they happen; learn from them and move on.

Another essential part of practicing humility is to never fall in love with your ideas. Be willing to change direction when data and experience tell you otherwise, and never ideologically commit to a marketing ideology, platform, or tactic. I have found having honest conversations with myself and colleagues about what campaigns can do realistically helps reduce the ridiculous expectation gaps between CEOs and CMOs and between clients and agencies.

When the Noise Is Loud, the Stakes Are Higher

Choose your hard. In marketing, you face two unavoidable challenges: letting go of bad ideas or letting them derail you. Choose wisely. Careers implode, client relationships sour, and strategies fail when professionals capitulate to uninformed demands and opinions, whether from the C-suite, clients, or their own teams. Remember, your job isn't to be liked; it's to be the calm, skeptical voice that stops the train from crashing, even if it means throwing yourself on the tracks. In a world drowning in "experts," platforms, and knee-jerk opinions, it's easy to confuse herd

ENOUGH ABOUT EVERYTHING GOING ON IN THE WORLD RIGHT NOW — WHAT'S **REALLY** IMPORTANT IS THE FONT SIZE OF THE HEADLINE OF OUR NEXT PROMOTION NO ONE WILL PAY ANY ATTENTION TO.

mentality activity with strategy. "Our competitors are on TikTok. Let's post videos!" "Two customers mentioned X. Let's overhaul our messaging!" "Sales are down. Let's sponsor my boss's bike race!" (Yes, that happened to me. No, I didn't comply. Yes, I got fired.)

This isn't just irrational; it's institutionalized delusion. Skepticism isn't cynicism; it's every marketer's armor against hype. Use it to dissect decisions: Why this platform? Why this message? Why this spend? Demand evidence and, as much as possible, not anecdotes.

A Case Study in Toxic Certainty

In 2021, we partnered with a small company launching a revolutionary product. The COO was a self-proclaimed "visionary" with a habit of citing his tenure at a well-known corporate giant who insisted on overruling our team based on his opinions. He'd derail strategies with irrelevant questions and force revisions to suit his ego, not what was best for the business. The CEO was too busy to get involved and when he did, he deferred to the COO. We faced a choice: fight every battle or focus on the launch as best we can. We chose the latter. On launch day, we secured coverage in a top financial publication and shared their article from a top business media site on the company's LinkedIn, a credibility boost for a fledgling brand and startup. The COO erupted, "Why is their logo here? Ours should be bigger!" He was referring to the logo of the business media company that LinkedIn automatically displays when sharing a link. His tantrum discounted, if not flat-out ignored, the strategic win. I told him to fire us. He didn't.

It's okay to not know everything. Ask questions, but trust the experts you hired. Confusing opinions with insight isn't leadership; it's sabotage. Marketing thrives on a simple rule: complex problems rarely have simple answers. Yet we're pressured to deliver both, often by those who prioritize comfort over results. Here's your antidote:

1. Interrogate every assumption (yes, even yours).

2. Model scenarios. What if we're wrong? What if two or three things were true at the same time?

3. Test relentlessly, even on a shoestring budget.

4. Execute with conviction, monitor outcomes, and adjust. I don't care if my skepticism makes you squirm. My goal isn't to soothe egos; it's to build campaigns that work. Bad ideas die in the light of scrutiny.

5

Play Fast. Play Smart.

Today, agility matters more than ever before. Depending on the lifecycle of your brand or your marketing objectives, you'll need to choose how you deploy your strategy, resources, and the pace of its campaign. Herm Edwards, former head coach of the New York Jets, famously declared, "You play to win the game." Being competitive means you must find ways to win and be able to map multiple paths to victory. In basketball, it's about the "next play mentality." As I mentioned earlier, if there's turnover, get back to play defense and get the ball back. Building on our humility discussion, seasoned competitors know how to lose, and, in many ways, every unsuccessful campaign should be examined fully and represents a learning situation to do better next time. Good coaches and players watch tape after the game. Every campaign should have a tape session.

Unsuccessful campaigns should have one of two paths: either drop them or adjust the campaign. Dropping it quickly can mean a situational and momentary loss, but not the game. Marketing misfires happen to all of us. Everyone from the likes of Nike, Apple, and Budweiser to startups and mom-and-pop shops suffer from misfires. While misfires are part and parcel of the business, the important thing is how to handle them. There's no shame in adjusting whenever the opportunity arises and, in some cases, it may mean cutting your losses. Michael Jordan said, "I've missed more than nine thousand shots in my career. I've lost almost three hundred games. Twenty-six times, I've been trusted to take the game-winning shot and missed. I've failed over and over and over again in my life. And that is why I succeed." We all should bring that perspective and determination to every engagement and every campaign.

Competing means respecting the game and the competition by being prepared. I don't just mean stuff like knowing your product, the market, platforms, pricing, macro forces, and competition; I mean your organization, sales teams, centers of influence, partners, agencies, products, services, and every nook and cranny of your business. You simply can't compete if you're not prepared, no matter how talented or smart you are. Preparedness allows you to be a steadfast advocate externally for your brand and an internal ally of leadership.

Be a Fiduciary: It's About More Than Money and Opportunity

One of the ways CMOs and agencies can close the trust gap with the executive suite is to practice transparency. Part of that is to act as a fiduciary, meaning being careful and strategic about marketing spend as if it's your own. I've advocated for a fiduciary approach because I was on the buy-side and it's how we run Verasoni now. Marketing and advertising were a blackbox before digital and in many ways they still are. Hidden agency fees and mark-ups on media buys are only two sources of irritation in the grand scheme of marketing. When I told some colleagues that Verasoni will not be up-charging or taking commission from media outlets and will pass those costs through as net to the client, some laughed and others were astonished: "You're leaving a lot of money on the table!" I may have left a lot of money on the table, but our client turnover is very low, and our client retention is about 8 years. I attribute that to our commitment to transparency and our fiduciary approach. In a May 2024 piece, Digiday discussed this very subject in examining the financial relationships between agencies and business: "When CMOs suspect agencies are profiting off of their ad spend, they often become uneasy. Typically, this leads to audits, hiring consultants, and publicly expressing frustrations about agencies covertly earning margins on their ad dollars. So, when a recent ANA report highlighted how major agency holding companies profit from media sales to clients, there was an expectation of a significant uproar."[37] We understand everyone must eat and it's good business to maximize profit, but when I was on the inside many moons ago, I was frustrated by the blackbox in traditional media, now exasperated in the digital age. So, it's right that CMOs should feel uneasy. The issue here is transparency.

Whether you're a CMO, in-house marketing team, or external agency, acting like a fiduciary sends a strong signal of transparency and partnership to your C-Suite and clients. It tells them you recognize your marketing responsibilities, including being a good steward of your marketing budget. That doesn't mean you shouldn't take risks or be opportunistic. Though, when you combine a fiduciary approach with humility and performance, it becomes a powerful foundation for trust. Even the most common-sense marketing budgets are sometimes perceived to be inflated by business leaders, and that's why marketing strategy needs to be focused and based on sound business principles. This requires lots of preparation, honesty about the lifecycle of the business, and marrying what's possible creatively with a responsible budget.

This approach is tightly connected to the marketing ethics we subscribe to at Verasoni. You'd think businesses would scamper to work with us because of this, but in fact, this approach has cost opportunity because the market is used to hearing something else more consistently.

Here's our creed (not apologizing for the commercial here, because I believe everyone should work in this manner):

1. **Always work in our clients' best interest.** We are interested in tactics and strategies that positively impact our clients' business, even if they are challenging to us.

2. **Honesty and transparency.** We are honest and transparent in everything we do. We will not misrepresent our or any products or services, exaggerate benefits, or make false claims.

3. **Responsibility.** We take responsibility for our actions and the impact they have on our clients and society. We will not engage in unethical practices that could harm our clients, individuals, or communities.

4. **Respect for intellectual property.** We respect intellectual property rights and do not engage in plagiarism, copyright infringement, or other unethical practices.

5. **Environmental responsibility.** We are aware of the impact our actions have on our environment and take steps to contribute to improving our planet.

6. **Social responsibility.** We are aware of the impact our actions have on society and act to contribute positively to communities.

7. **Continuous improvement.** We continuously improve our knowledge and skills to ensure that we are up to date with the latest ethical practices and marketing standards that allow us to give the best possible advice to our clients, saving them time and money.

8. **We act like a fiduciary.** We recognize clients trust us with their hard-earned capital and we promise to be good stewards of those funds, fully recognizing that not everything we do will work.

The above is meant to be shared, so if this works for you, go ahead and copy it, or add to it to make it your own. It's living those values that can contribute to reducing the trust gap between marketers and everyone else.

Organizational Dynamics and Marketing Tools

If you're working in a corporate setting, selling to corporate, or part of a large team from a startup to a multinational corporation, pay attention. As discussed earlier, unlike accounting or other business disciplines, virtually everyone fancies themselves a marketing expert. And why not? Marketing is fun and creative, and everyone likes to think they're creative. People who watch TV come to believe they can produce TV commercials, and people who have Facebook accounts are social media aficionados, right?

Defining the Marketing Infrastructure and Technology Stack

From small local businesses to multinational corporations, the importance of selecting the right marketing technologies can't be overstated. Well-chosen marketing technologies are important tools to deploy, design, and track campaigns. For businesses with limited resources, this can mean getting more done with less. The right marketing tech stack helps maximize marketing efficiency and productivity.

Marketing is a symphony, each instrument playing an important role. Your tech stack is a collection of software tools and platforms that come together to enable your marketing campaigns and allow you to orchestrate your strategies. A marketing tech stack includes but is not limited to:

- Customer relationship management (CRM)
- Email system
- Voiceover IP phone system
- Analytics dashboard
- Social media dashboard
- Website content management system
- Reviews system
- SMS

Seamless Integration Is Important but Nuances Matter

Your marketing systems—CRM, lead capture forms, email automation— must work as a unified engine, not isolated tools. For example, syncing your website's contact forms with HubSpot CRM instantly routes leads into sales pipelines, triggers personalized email sequences, and turns raw data into actionable insights. This isn't just convenience; it's operational oxygen for modern marketing.

A tech stack is a strategy, not a shopping list. A well-designed stack does three things:

1. Eliminates friction.
2. Captures golden data.
3. Delivers precision.

The reality is technology doesn't build strategy; strategy builds technology. Tools like HubSpot or Marketo are enablers, not saviors. You can own the shiniest stack in the room, but without teams who wield it ruthlessly (and know when to ignore it), you're just paying for shelfware. So, align your stack with long-term goals, but stay nimble. Avoid multi-year platform commitments, as today's "must-have" AI widget could be obsolete in 18 months. Invest in talent, not tools. Train teams to think and adapt, not just operate software.

The reality is marketing tech tools don't create advantage; people do. Your competitive edge isn't your CRM's features; it's the people behind your CRM who know when and how to automate and when to pick up the phone. Technology scales effort. Judgment scales results.

Here's how we select marketing stacks for our clients:

1. **Define goals and assess needs.** Start by clearly outlining your business objectives and organizational complexities, and assess the talent and experience of the marketing professionals in the department. Clarify your goals to help identify the tools that align with the desired outcomes. If and where there's a deficit, fill it with training or by buying or renting talent. For example, if we don't have the necessary talent to implement Salesforce or HubSpot, we'll hire a contractor. We will ask the contractor to document the work so we have institutional knowledge. We will also conduct a thorough analysis of marketing processes to determine business goals for the tech stack, what gaps exist, and what best-in-class technologies we can use.

2. **Scalability and flexibility.** Any marketing tech stack must be scalable to ensure that these tools can grow and adapt with your business. This is particularly important for startups and growing companies that need a solution that can accommodate their changing needs without requiring a complete overhaul.

3. **Budget consideration.** This stuff costs money. Your budget alone will shape your marketing technology stack. Don't chase the latest shiny tool; ensure that the cost aligns with the value it brings to your business. You may

think you need a CRM when you only need a good email partner. Consider both the upfront expenses and ongoing subscription costs.

4. **Integration capability.** Choose technology tools that can seamlessly integrate with one another, reducing data silos and helping to streamline your operations. For example, does your CRM integrate with your website and email client?

5. **Customer support.** We choose platforms with responsive customer support to ensure we're making the most of your investment, and sometimes that means paying a little more.

6. **Prioritize security and compliance.** In an age of data breaches and increasing privacy concerns, security is paramount. We select tools, to the extent possible, that prioritize data protection and comply with relevant regulations.

7. **Test and evaluate.** Before fully committing to a tool, we test it through trials, demos, or pilot projects. This provides valuable insights into its compatibility with workflows and how well it delivers on its promises.

Marketing Expectations Are Kinda Insane, No?

Aside from managing the necessary moving parts to keep marketing aligned with your business goals, an important part of marketing is setting realistic expectations for you and your business. Marketers can relate to what I'm about to say next. Sales are down—"Where's marketing?" Market is down—"Cut marketing." A recession is coming and numbers are down this month—"What's marketing doing?" Our competition is going viral and we're not and their CEO is on TV climbing Everest with a sherpa—"Why isn't ours?" And those 5 a.m. emails from your CFO who "just read about" something and needed to share their thoughts.

While this is part of the dynamics of any job, I welcome these opportunities to engage and talk all things marketing with team members and business leaders. Assuming marketing is thoughtful and doing a good job, marketing detractors in organizations can be tiresome and affect moral. I think of it this way: since people are drawn to marketing, there's an opportunity to engage your coworkers, whether they're critics or supporters of your work. Yet, there's no question that one should draw a line on the involvement of your coworkers because their opinions and feelings may be important to them but should not be to you. Ultimately, marketing democracy or by committee is marketing mediocrity. Don't put up with it. You can continue to be a team player, engaging colleagues and stakeholders on your terms by educating them along the way.

Aligning your organization with your marketing intention isn't always easy, especially in today's environment, which can easily foment FOMO among colleagues. Start with transparency to build trust in what you do and how to do it. In the next chapter, we'll delve into the fundamentals of building a smarter approach to marketing, which ultimately contributes to building trust in your strategies and approach.

6 Fundamentals for the Win

Flashy plays in pro or college sports come along occasionally, and when they do, they're breathtaking! Sometimes there are several in a game. It's the impossible shot in tennis, the deep bomb after a fake handoff in football for a one-handed-grab touchdown, or the no-look-behind-the-back pass for a crowd-roaring dunk in basketball. Sometimes these plays are planned, but many times they're pure luck. Right place, right time kind of thing. While they're spectacular to watch, they are essentially micro-moments in a much larger, longer, and more complex game that is won or lost on executing fundamentals.

The same is true with marketing. Fundamentals, boring as they may be, are always at the cornerstone of any marketing win. Occasionally campaigns score a memorable play, usually by already famous brands. When marketers see something good, especially by big brands, they'll try to replicate it. But big brands are like super-athletes armed with outsized budgets, influence, and maybe talent. When you have big budgets, you're bound to hit a grand slam at the bottom of the ninth!

Regardless, cool marketing campaigns from big budget brands are fun to watch, though marketing mortals with smaller budgets and big ambitions should always rely on fundamental principles of the game, because most of it is played that way.

Principle 1: Marketing Is Fundamentally Human

Let's cut through the noise because algorithms don't buy products; people do. Marketing's greatest irony? It appears that right now we're chasing platforms, data, and generational labels like Gen Z and Millennials, but we forget the only acronym that matters: H2H (*human to human*). Every transaction, from a teenager scrolling Twitch to a CFO negotiating a SaaS contract, boils down to one primal truth: *people buy from people.* Even the slickest tech is just a middleman in a conversation that's always been between us.

Take Burger King's 2017 Halloween stunt, a masterclass in human psychology. By weaponizing Google Trends (clown costumes were surging) and trolling McDonald's iconic mascot, they offered free Whoppers to anyone dressed as a clown. The results were outstanding! 2.1 billion impressions. $22.4 million in earned media. Not because of TikTok ads or hyper-targeting, but because they tapped into something visceral: our love of mischief, nostalgia, and free stuff.

The lesson here is behavioral insight is your North Star. Platforms change. Algorithms evolve. But humans? We've been craving connection, status, and solutions since we bartered rugs for grain.

So here's your challenge: stop fetishizing "digital" vs. "legacy." Start asking:

- What makes my audience feel seen?
- What unspoken desire does my product answer?
- How do I turn transactions into relationships?

The future belongs to marketers who remember that bots might optimize clicks, but humans build empires. The next time someone says, "AI will replace marketers," remind them robots don't crave Whoppers.

Principle 2: Be Persuasive; Master Influence

We live in an era of content hyperproduction, a relentless, mechanized churn of posts, ads, and campaigns that would make Henry Ford's assembly lines blush. Every minute, 500 hours of video surge onto YouTube. Over 350 million photos flood Instagram daily. LinkedIn users publish 2 million articles a week. This is an industrialized distraction, a dystopian factory where marketers toil as digital serfs, mining fleeting engagement for algorithmic overlords. These folks are praying for virality, chasing trends like dogs after cars, and shovel more coal into the furnace of an insatiable machine.

Let's be honest, most of this content isn't persuasive; it's landfill material. It's just there. For legacy brands, this noise is survivable. Coca-Cola could post a blank red can and rack up millions of views and get people to talk about its meaning. Apple's logo alone sparks flurries of speculation. Their privilege? Cultural ubiquity and fame. Established brands don't need persuasion; they need presence.

For everyone else—the startups, the challengers, the underdogs— the game is rigged. Imagine a bootstrapped skincare startup competing with L'Oréal's TikTok budget. Or a climate-tech nonprofit shouting into the void against Shell's greenwashed billions. These Davids aren't fighting Goliaths; they're battling tsunamis with tablespoons. It's not impossible, but it is improbable.

Liquid Death is one of those impossible brands. The canned water brand hijacked heavy metal aesthetics to mock beverage industry tropes. With a mere fraction of Coca-Cola's budget, they turned hydration into a middle finger to corporate blandness. Their secret? Bold, unapologetic persuasion. A viral video of a "murdered" plastic bottle (chainsaw included) wasn't just content but a cultural splash. Liquid Death didn't beg for attention; they boldly seized it.

Consider Oatly, the rebel oat milk company. Facing dairy industry Goliaths, they scrawled irreverent rants on NYC dumpsters and wheat-pasted posters with headlines like "It's like milk but made for humans." No influencers. No pre-roll ads. Just guerrilla wit that dared commuters to stop and think. In seconds, they reframed a commodity into a manifesto that connected and persuaded buyers.

Today, persuasion is about voltage. Marketers keep feeding the beast, mistaking activity for impact. We're trapped in a circus of distraction, TikTok dances, LinkedIn platitudes, and Instagram reels that vanish faster than a Snapchat story. "Oh look, squirrel!" has become our cultural mantra.

The antidote is simply to refuse to play the factory's game, and that's hard. But in the process, think of it like this:

- Forget virality. Chase cultural resonance.
- Ditch trends. Build unignorable ideas.
- Burn the "best practices" handbook. Replace it with audacity.

Principle 3: Branding—Building Your Brand Mythology

People buy products all the time, but things change dramatically when they buy a product with a story. Branding is a tempting elixir that puts your buyer into a loyalty trance by forging a tight connection (emotional, logical, or some other type) to your products or services. Branding gives the answer to "I buy this product over and over because...." Branding is the mythology created from your customers experiencing your brand over time. It is the story you tell your customers, which then gets translated into the story that customers tell themselves about why they buy and what they feel about your stuff. Why do you buy Apple, Nike, or any brand you like? What mythology would you like to create for your business?

Storytelling is as intrinsic to brand myth and design as the product or service themselves. Brand mythology can serve as a source of inspiration and provide a profound sense of identity. The Starbucks story isn't necessarily about good coffee. Starbucks legendary mythology takes its customers to another world. Think about this: Americans for the most part don't gravitate to foreign languages. Yet Starbucks has managed to teach its customers to order coffee in a foreign language. What will you have? Grande, venti, or trenta? They're friggin' ordering coffee, not doing trigonometry in Latin! Indeed, that's one part of Starbucks brand mythology. People may feel better or cooler when they order a "grande" rather than a "large." Ordering coffee at Starbucks is an entirely different experience than ordering coffee at your local diner. In another example, while Nike built a fortune on Michael Jordan's brand, the brand's mythology in its early days was led by Mars Blackmon, a quirky, relatable, loveable character created by Spike Lee in the 1980s. In a series of iconic TV ads, Mars Blackmon deduced that Jordan's basketball prowess was intrinsically connected to his footwear, because "It's gotta be the shoes." In both cases, the mythology successfully connected with customers and created a feeling about the brands. When their customers internalized that feeling, that's when the brand captured the human mind and spirit.

> **"Marketing is no longer about the stuff you make, but the stories you tell. And stories are hard because they require empathy, not just data."**
>
> —Seth Godin, marketing guru and author of *This Is Marketing* (2018)

Myths can be created about any business, not just global brands. I live in northern New Jersey, and there's a local legend that the best pizza in the state, if not the country, is at the Star Tavern in Orange, New Jersey. For years, people have said, "You've got to go to the Star Tavern! They have the best pizza!" I'd respond, "I'd love to! When was the last time you went?" And they'll say, "Oh, I haven't been, but people keep saying how good it is." So, let me get this straight: people are recommending a pizza place they've never been to because they've "heard" it was the best pizza from other people? Now that's brand power and mythology working in overdrive! When I finally visited the Star Tavern, my taste buds high-fived. It was that good! My goodness, the pizza was terrific! Today, the Star Tavern's legend continues to thrive in our area.

Let's take another example that's close to my heart: America, or the idea of America. I believe the United States of America is the most powerful brand on Earth. Not Coke, not Nike, not Facebook. It's the United States of America. The distribution of American values, and by extension its brand, began in earnest right after the United States abandoned its doctrine of neutrality to enter World War I. As America's brand and global influence gained speed in the years to come, its businesses rode the same wave to international expansion and global domination enjoyed by no nation in history. There isn't a back corner on this globe where one can't get a Coke or an iPhone. American movies and music are piped into the most remote areas of the globe, where Keanu Reeves, Merryl Streep, and Angelina Jolie are practically household names.

As I mentioned earlier, growing up in Aleppo in the 1970s, American products were everywhere, despite Syria's alignment with the old Soviet Union. While I can't remember a single Soviet product during my time there, I fell in love with Batman, Superman, Nancy Drew, and the Hardy Boys. I watched *The Virginian*, *The Six-Million Dollar Man*, and played Cowboys and Indians on Aleppo's ancient streets with friends. I often indulged in a cold 7Up, Coke, or Pepsi to cool off in the stubbornly hot summers. I learned about Cadillac and Jimmy Carter from the adults around me. With every sip of Pepsi, every episode of *Little House on the Prairie*, I experienced, and to a certain extent lived, the American brand and everything it stood for. Through everything I was exposed to that was American, I came to perceive American culture as open and innovative. America was a place for liberty, equality, justice. That's what Batman and Superman told me. My perception about America was formed by consuming Americans ideas from the multitude of movies and TV shows I watched, the products we bought, and the stories told to us by people who visited or immigrated to the States. So, even though I'd never been to America, nor did I speak English at the time, I felt its power and presence from six thousand miles away. I connected with America by watching Bugs Bunny and Woody Woodpecker with Arabic subtitles. Pre-internet and social media, people experienced America's brand through entertainment, products, and even postcards that inspired many from around the world to immigrate to "the land of milk and honey where streets are paved with gold," according to my good friend and former sociology professor, the late Phil Kayal, PhD, Professor Emeritus at Seton Hall University. In class one day, Dr. Kayal made an observation about how badly the Irish in America were treated in the late 19th and early 20th centuries. Like many newcomers to the United States, Irish immigrants faced many hostilities, including violence and job discrimination. "Irish need not apply" was a popular line in classified ads and on signs in storefronts. "But as soon as they integrated into American society, as soon as they were accepted, they named a soap after them. Irish Spring!" As Dr. Kayal preached from behind the lectern, the entire class roared with laughter, with many in the class clapping at the truth bomb. Go back to what I shared earlier about the concept of *when* is your brand. Irish Spring would have never come close to being a marketable product during the time of Irish persecution in the U.S. But it had its moment decades later only after Irish assimilation and societal acceptance of the group.

Whether it's America, Nike, the Star Tavern, Irish Americans, or Irish Spring, the process of branding has no precise recipe or formula, though many of its ingredients can be identified. There are fundamental attributes that make great brands, but the elements of one brand's successful journey may not at all necessarily be reflective in another's, and the formula for their success can be quite unique and not exactly duplicatable. For example, one can't compare the rate of adoption of Apple's brand versus Coke because, aside from being in vastly different sectors, their lifecycle is vastly different. The moments in which they rose were just right to allow them to flourish. Yet when we examine their brand attributes, there are similarities that jump right at us, including but not limited to:

- Beloved products, service, ideas.
- Emotional storytellers.
- Dedicated and flexible budget.
- Leverage out of industry partnerships.
- Consistent, never out of the market.
- Stay culturally relevant.
- Innovative.

In the case of Apple and Coke, both companies have shaped their respective destinies by carefully and consistently controlling the stories they told about themselves. How, why, and how fast you emotionally connect to those brands is an important part of the branding calculus, but no one knows how long it will take for a successful brand to get a foothold on its customer base or culture.

Branding today exists in a peculiar duality: its essence remains rooted in age-old principles, yet the landscape it inhabits has transformed into a frenetic, fragmented arena. Audiences scatter across countless platforms, markets shift at dizzying speeds, and marketers cling to jargon like "brand purpose" or "community-building" as lifelines. Amid this chaos, voices like Paul Feldwick and Bob Hoffman cut through the noise with a radical yet refreshing argument, that branding's most potent force isn't complexity, but fame.

Feldwick, in his book *Why Does the Peddler Sing?*, dismisses the modern obsession with convoluted frameworks, positioning statements, value essences, purpose-driven manifestos. Instead, he champions fame as the cornerstone of brand success. "Marketers tie themselves in knots over layers of theory," he writes, "while overlooking the simplest truth: fame isn't about ideals or slogans. It's about being known, remembered, and relentlessly discussed." Bob Hoffman, the sharp-tongued "Ad Contrarian," echoes this bluntly. He mocks the industry's romantic delusions—consumers craving "relationships" with brands or joining "tribes"—as largely fantasy. "The most reliable driver of success isn't purpose or meaning," he argues. "It's fame. Not a guarantee, but the closest thing to a sure bet."

There's something to Bob's take that rings true if you look close enough. Take Tommy Hilfiger's rise to fame, which was fueled by audacious marketing, cultural intuition, and a knack for reinventing classic American style. Starting as a teenage entrepreneur with a small boutique in upstate New York, he honed his understanding of youth trends before launching his namesake brand in 1985 with a brash Times Square billboard that provocatively positioned him among fashion giants like Ralph Lauren and Calvin Klein. This bold stunt sparked controversy but cemented his rebellious, aspirational image. His breakthrough came in the 1990s when he embraced hip-hop culture, a then-undervalued force in mainstream fashion. Artists like Snoop Dogg and Aaliyah donned his oversized, logo-driven designs, transforming Hilfiger into a streetwear icon and bridging high fashion with urban cool. Doubling down on fame through strategic collaborations and celebrity endorsements, Hilfiger's genius lay in telling everyone he was already famous, even when he wasn't yet, a formula that turned his name into a billion-dollar empire. How about when Ryan Reynolds and Rob McElhenney's Hollywood star power transformed Wrexham AFC from a struggling fifth-tier Welsh football club into a global phenomenon, proving that celebrity can rewrite underdog narratives and uplift downtrodden brands. Their ownership became a masterclass in modern branding: leveraging their massive social media followings (Reynolds' 21 million Twitter/X followers, McElhenney's *It's Always Sunny in Philadelphia* fanbase) to amplify the club's profile, they turned matches into must-watch events and jerseys into cult collectibles. The docuseries *Welcome to Wrexham*, a heartfelt chronicle of their ownership journey, drew millions of viewers on FX and Hulu, humanizing the team's quest for promotion while spotlighting the town's working-class spirit. This exposure fueled a 400-percent spike in merchandise sales, while sponsors like TikTok, Aviation Gin, and Expedia clamored to partner with the suddenly viral club. Their playful marketing genius shone in stunts like Reynolds challenging fans to a crossbar TikTok contest (offering free gin for life) and McElhenney rallying Philadelphia Eagles fans to adopt Wrexham as their "second team." Crucially, their fame wasn't just a megaphone; it funded progress. Revenue from sponsorships and documentary deals helped sign key players, renovate the stadium, and invest in community projects, culminating in Wrexham's 2023 promotion after a 15-year drought. By blending A-list fame with grassroots authenticity, they turned a local team into a global symbol of hope, and proved that sometimes, fairy tales do have Hollywood endings.

What is fame? It's the raw power of cultural ubiquity. Apple's "1984" commercial or Nike's Just Do It fit the bill. These campaigns didn't thrive on meticulously crafted brand guidelines or emotional storytelling alone. They became indelible because they saturated culture, transforming brands into shared, inescapable, undeniable references. Fame isn't about being loved; it's about being unforgettable.

Yet fame is no panacea. Hoffman cautions that even iconic brands stumble, like Coca-Cola's New Coke debacle or Gap's ill-fated logo redesign. "Famous brands fail all the time," he admits. "But in a world of probabilities, it's still the strongest hand to play." The lesson isn't to chase fame blindly, but to recognize its unmatched leverage.

So, discard the playbooks overstuffed with jargon. Ask instead: Does your brand cut through the static? Is it talked about, debated, mimicked? In an era of endless noise, fame isn't vanity; it's a flex. It boxes the competition in certain respects. Purpose fades and trends evaporate. But being impossible to ignore? That's forever.

No two ways about it: creating brand myths and making brands famous are time consuming, expensive, and improbable for many. Any serious thought about creating brand mythology must include a long-term horizon. Full stop. Brand mythology isn't for the faint of heart. Brands must be ready to sustain and even grow their investment in mythology. I'm often asked about using social media to build brands with people citing the rags to riches story of Khloé Kardashian. Astonishingly, well-meaning marketing professionals have used that specific example many times. My response is Khloé, like her sister Kim, was famous offline before she was famous in the digital space. Khloé first gained fame and wealth through the reality TV show *Keeping Up with the Kardashians*. The show's 20-season run was a massive success, making Khloé and her family household names. She also appeared in several spin-offs, including *Kourtney and Khloé Take Miami* and *Khloé & Lamar*. She simply translated her offline fame online. It was TV that drove her digital success. Therefore, it's easier for already established brands like Dunkin' or Wendy's, who have already found fame offline, to gain traction and find brand mythology success on social media than startups. That doesn't mean that startups can't find success on social platforms, but it's simply easier for already famous brands to project on social.

> **"Reputation, reputation! Oh, I have lost my reputation! I have lost the immortal part of myself and what remains is bestial."**
>
> —William Shakespeare, *Othello*

Making brands famous is one thing; keeping them famous is another. Both require money and talent. Speaking of fame and money, let's take Americans' perception of our healthcare system, which commands almost 20 percent of the U.S. GDP. Although the healthcare system as a whole doesn't invest in its brand mythology, it is "famous" in the U.S. for being "the best." It's a confluence of many things that come together to build the healthcare system's reputation, including American exceptionalism, political leadership, individual hospitals spending on marketing, physician practice marketing, and medical school reputation, among other factors. The point is the system as a whole spends nothing (time, money) on its brand mythology. Though, it's a safe bet to say Americans like to complain about their health system while at the same time fiercely defending it as the best healthcare system in the world. But a peek under the covers here tells a vastly different story than what Americans have come to believe about the brand of their healthcare.

According to Peterson-KFF Health System Tracker, "Despite spending more money per capita on healthcare than any similarly large and wealthy nation, the United States has a lower life expectancy than peer nations and has seen worsening health outcomes since the onset of the COVID-19 pandemic." The same study shows Americans have more heart attacks and strokes than comparable countries.[38] With respect to maternal deaths, "The United States continues to have the highest rate of maternal deaths of any high-income nation," according to the Commonwealth Fund.[39] By many measures, many credible studies show that the American healthcare system costs Americans more and delivers less than any healthcare system in the world comparatively. So, why do Americans continue to believe that their healthcare system stands tallest when its performance is pathetic? Branding. There isn't one attribute that can explain this phenomenon, but politicians, doctors, and the media, along with the entertainment industry, like doctor shows, sing a steady song of praises of the healthcare system, creating its mythology. At the same time, mythologies about alternative healthcare options and systems in Canada and Europe are created and delivered with similar vigor and branded as "socialized medicine," essentially gaslighting the public. The intersections, and there are many, of praise for the American system and demonizing the systems of others through frequency and placement of seemingly randomly but well-orchestrated messaging creates an emotional connection that is crucial to building the brand mythology around the American healthcare system. The mythology tells people to suspend reality and their actual experience with the American healthcare system. Besides, who wants to admit that the American healthcare system, or even parts of it, is both expensive and ineffective, even if there's data to support that position?

This may sound ruthless to many, but I will ask you to fade your feelings for a dose of reality: I consider well-executed gaslighting campaigns excellent branding. Because they are. This is neither good nor bad; it just is. Let's examine American politics. Take the Republican Party's claims on fiscal responsibility and the Democrats' claims on reeling in corporate interests. Both are fundamentally untrue yet are perpetuated by party faithful and political backseat drivers alike. But the success of myths like we just discussed is connected to the storytellers themselves, their platform, the frequency of message, and the emotional investment the audience has in the subject, which goes back to their perception of the messenger, their exposure to platforms and media that deliver these messages, and how often they hear the same message. In all this, storytelling and the storytellers are key. Anytime a campaign pulls in the audience to internalize the message and connect it to their own belief system, the brand can strike gold.

The Alchemy of Obsession: Successful Brands Hijack Hearts, Not Minds

Great branding isn't a transaction; it's a process. When a brand claws its way into the gut of its audience and further up into the heart, it creates a home. The myth becomes a creed, then a tattoo on the spirit that no logic nor laser can scrub clean. Apple isn't a tech company; it's a cult of cool defiance. Nike isn't footwear; it's a rallying point for the relentless. These brands don't ask for loyalty; they command it, turning customers into (sometimes mindless) apostles who evangelize not because of features or quality but because of feeling. Think of the New York Knicks, a franchise synonymous with mediocrity for the past 20 years or so, yet their tickets at Madison Square Garden sell like Star Tavern pizza. Fans don't rationalize, "This team is worth $750 a seat." They bleed orange and blue because the Knicks aren't a basketball team; they're a battered, generational heirloom where rationality is irrelevant. The brain is a bystander here, watching as the heart howls, "This is who we are."

Gucci is another example of a $3,000 Dionysian fever dream draped in leather and audacity. No one needs a snake-embossed handbag. But need is not the point. Gucci sells delirium, the thrill of being seen as someone unapologetically excessive, someone who laughs at practicality. And CNN? You don't "agree" with CNN. You rage at it, or you trust it like a weathered parent. There's no middle ground. Neutrality is death for brands.

When Apple launches an ad, it's not selling a phone; it's selling a manifesto: "Join the enlightened." When Nike slaps "Just Do It" on a shoe, it's not footwear; it's a shove into the arena of cultural relevancy and in many ways, conformity. Here's the brutal calculus of modern branding: Weak brands beg for attention with discounts and hashtags. Legendary brands rewire human desire. Great branding isn't marketing. It's psychological alchemy. The Knicks' losing streak? Irrelevant. Gucci's impracticality? A feature, not a bug. CNN's or Fox News's polarization? Proof they're alive. These brands thrive because they don't target wallets; they target identity. They whisper (or scream), "This is who you could be. This is who you already are." So ask yourself: Does your brand settle for clicks, or does it demand conviction? Are you filling carts and taking orders, or are you filling voids? In the end, we don't choose brands. They choose us by hijacking our hearts before our brains can mutter a word of protest.

> **"The Party told you to reject the evidence of your eyes and ears. It was their final, most essential command."**
> —George Orwell, *1984*

It's only over time that people develop feelings and emotions about products, services, and ideas. Because people need to experience the brand, and that takes time. So the time element is pivotal, and we'll get to that later in this chapter. Somehow, especially for SMBs, the middle market, and even for some larger players, branding has become about content development, logos, websites, advertising, or social posts. Brands that endure understand branding is about how your customers feel before, during, and after they interact with your brand. Remember, it took years for Coca-Cola and Jersey Mike's to become brands. Both were and are bolstered by products people want and reinforced by consistent, unrelenting marketing and advertising strategies. Good brand managers tap into time and emotions, which are natural human constructs.

Principle 4: Relevancy Through Consistency

What makes St. Jude Research Hospital one of the preeminent not-for-profit healthcare organizations in the world? Since its founding in 1962, St. Jude provides free cancer treatment to children and their families and is the living legacy of its founder, the beloved entertainer Danny Thomas. But to fulfill its mission, St. Jude's needs to stay relevant. It does so with consistent television and radio partnerships with high-profile celebrities, professional sports affiliations, and digital campaigns. They don't say, "Oh, we raised enough funds this year. Let's save some money by dropping advertising this year." They know their consistent presence and advertising position is connected to staying relevant in the minds of potential donors, keeping the organization top of mind and its mission alive in front of millions. In many ways, St. Jude's, as a brand and business, behaves like Ford, Target, and other national advertisers to say relevant in the minds of its current donors (customers) while acquiring new ones.

Even strong brands must recognize any new product or service they produce must be relevant to customers. Some of the best companies and brands introduce products that fall flat. Let's examine a few misses:

- **Coca-Cola.** New Coke is a classic case of one of greatest brand misses of all time. Launched in April 1985, New Coke was a reformulated version of Coca-Cola. The company created New Coke in response to declining sales and increasing competition from Pepsi. New Coke sparked a significant public backlash. Coca-Cola lovers were outraged by the change, with many expressing strong emotional devotion to the original formula. The backlash included protests, a flood of complaints to the company, and created a media frenzy. As a result, in only 79 days after the launch of New Coke, Coca-Cola announced the return of the original formula, branded as "Coca-Cola Classic." While New Coke went away quickly, Coke today is as strong as ever.

- **Google.** Google Glass flopped swiftly because product usability was difficult, and it confused the hell out of people to boot. Google Glass broke in about 20 months, and yet Google continues to be a juggernaut.

- **Amazon.** Ever heard of Amazon Restaurants? Amazon launched the same-day service that delivered freshly prepared food from local restaurants to Prime customers in 2015 and shut it down in 2018.

- **Frito Lay.** What about Cheetos' 2015 launch of Cheetos Lip Balm? Yeah, you read that right! Did Frito Lay, the PepsiCo subsidiary, think Cheetos Lip Balm would catch on? What were they thinking? Yet, despite the utter fiasco of that bright idea, Cheetos continues to be a beloved brand, but you won't find it in the lip balm section of your supermarket or drugstore.

Here are a few successes:

- **Toyota.** The company launched the Lexus brand in the late 1980s as part of a strategic initiative to enter the luxury automobile market, particularly targeting the U.S., where it was a formidable player. Known for its reliability, Toyota knew that its brand did not resonate with the luxury buyer, and it also knew luxury buyers drove Mercedes, Ferrari, BMW, and Porsche. Branding its luxury drive "Toyota xR70" will likely not be appealing because luxury drivers won't feel comfortable with saying "I drive a Toyota." So, Toyota created the Lexus brand, which allowed it to successfully compete with luxury brands.

- **Nintendo.** The company was founded in 1889 as a playing card company, and it became a major player in the video game industry by the 1980s, with iconic products and brands like the NES (Nintendo Entertainment System) and Game Boy. In 2006, the company introduced the Wii, a motion-controlled gaming console that was a significant departure from traditional gaming systems. The Wii's appeal to a broader audience, including non-gamers, parents, families, and seniors, helped sell over 100 million units worldwide and solidified Nintendo's reputation as an innovative leader in the industry.

- **Lego.** The building blocks company is a beloved global brand in children's toys around the world. In 1998, the company introduced Lego Mindstorms, a line of programmable robotics kits that combined Lego bricks with computer technology, allowing users to build and program robots. The product was an instant hit among hobbyists, educators, and students fostering interest in STEM (Science, Technology, Engineering, and Mathematics) fields and helped Lego stay relevant in the digital age.

Relevance isn't a buzzword; it's at the heart of your product, service, or idea. A brand's ability to *pulse* with the needs, desires, and values of its audience isn't just practical; it's existential. Brands that master this alchemy don't merely sell products. They embed themselves into the daily rhythms of life, becoming indispensable. Relevance is the currency of modern commerce. It's less about shouting louder or more often in a crowded market, and more about capturing the soul of your audience. When a brand consistently answers unmet cravings, solves unspoken frustrations, or mirrors evolving values, it forges something far stronger than loyalty: irreplaceability.

Look at a brand like Patagonia, threading environmental activism into every product, or Duolingo, turning language learning into a TikTok-era game. They don't just meet needs; they anticipate what is around the corner. The brand is active within and around its product and culture. So it's not surprising to see cult-like devotion, market dominance, and a gravitational pull that outmuscles competitors. But relevance is a ruthless and indifferent ally. Fail to evolve, and you become background noise, like Betamax. Ignore shifting cultural tides, and you drown in them, like Blockbuster. In the court of consumer choice, relevance is the only seat at the table.

Principle 5: Your Corporate Identity and Logos (Important, But Not as Important as You Think)

From startups to mature businesses, no one is immune to thinking about the importance of their logo or corporate identity. Startups fret at the start of their business and more mature companies when they launch new products, services, or sub-brands. In the grand scheme of things, your logo is your corporate identity and plays a small, but very important part of your brand, depending on how long that logo has been in the marketplace.

The classic case is Nike's iconic swoosh. The company wanted a simple logo that conveyed motion, but the logo itself was an exercise in graphic arts and didn't become pervasive until it found a catalyst. That catalyst was basketball superstar Michael Jordan, who helped Nike grow to become the most dominant brand in its space on the planet. Now, I often wonder what the impact of Nike's logo would have been if Michael Jordan didn't come along, or if he signed with Adidas like he was supposed to. Luckily for Nike and much to the chagrin of Adidas, that scenario is fodder for our imagination. Nike's logo was created in 1971 but didn't become relevant until about 1984, 13 years later. It would be foolish to argue that Nike's logo propelled the company to global dominance. It didn't. The popularity of the logo is a consequence of many things, including its affiliation with Michael Jordan. If your corporate identity is appropriate and the best it can be right now, move on to more important things. You have bigger fish to fry.

No one ever looks at Dell's logo and says, "I'm not buying a computer from those guys. The E is crooked in their logo." No one drives by McDonald's and thinks, "Damn I hate that M." Of course not. The truth is businesses care more about their logo than their customers do. No one ever wakes up and thinks about logos or brands. Sure, Apple has incredible brand equity in its logo, which happened over time, but startups aren't afforded the same luxury as established brands. Neither do middle market companies who dabble in logo design. For goodness' sake, Johnson & Johnson replaced its iconic logo font with, in my opinion, an offensively hideous font logo. Do I believe it will improve their business in any way? No. Do I believe it will hurt their business? No. Your logo or corporate identity, like your brand, is only relevant if you continue to make it relevant (see Principle 3 on page 112).

Yet many companies that could benefit from rebranding are reluctant to consider the idea. Founder-led brands (Virgin's Branson, Tesla's Musk) thrive on personality as product, a cult of charisma where the founder's DNA is the brand. Legacy brands (Ford, IBM) leverage longevity and perseverance as a silent promise: "We outlived trends; we've outlived wars and recessions; we'll outlive your doubts." But something else has happened recently: revered brands like the aforementioned Johnson & Johnson and Jaguar ditched their beloved logos, replacing them with simple fonts. It's because they recognized that nostalgia in their corporate identity may be oversold in a time of dizzying access to brands by consumers. Businesses would do well to remember that legacy isn't inherited; it's earned and claimed.

Rebranding can be expensive and risky if not done and rolled out in a meaningful way. Just ask Facebook, whose name change to Meta didn't go smoothly because Meta means "dead" or "he's dead" for the 400 million Arabic speakers on the planet. More recently, KIA's new logo is cool, but created some confusion where people were Googling "KN" cars, rather than KIA. Rebranding requires complete focus on why to rebrand first, regardless of the size of your company. Here are some questions to ponder:

- What is the purpose of rebranding?
- Is there a market or product catalyst for the rebrand? If there isn't, what would be the story for the rebrand?
- What do we rebrand? The name of the business or our corporate DNA? Both?
- What value is there in the current name and/or logo and what value do we expect to derive from the new?
- Can we use this opportunity to engage and reengage our customers?
- How do we leverage the rebrand into getting our customers and market partners excited about our efforts across platforms?

Consider that some of the world's most iconic companies with tremendous brand equity rebranded recently. Rebranding comes in various shades, of course. The two most popular rebranding approaches are the name change, which always comes with a new logo, and the logo-only rebrand. In January 2019, the world's most popular donut brand, Dunkin' Donuts, changed its name to Dunkin'. Also in 2019, E-bates changed its name to Rakuten to reflect the Japanese company's takeover of Ebates. Let that sink in—going from the simple Ebates to the insanely complicated RA-KOO-TIN. But to their credit, they succeeded through a series of TV commercials and cross platforms ads that playfully taught the market how to say their new name and subsequent, continued messaging of the name.

> "To me, marketing is about values. A great brand starts with a great product, but it's the story you wrap around it that makes people care."
>
> —Steve Jobs, Apple's Think Different campaign launch (1997)

There's a long list of companies who have relatively recently changed their corporate identity or logos, including Netflix, Verizon, and Uber. Each has their own strategic reasons for the new look. When we work with clients, we favor simple, unambiguous logos and corporate identity—the simpler, the better. With all the competition for attention across digital and traditional platforms, simple logos cut through the clutter and have the advantage and potential for sustainability and longevity. Think about font-based logos like Morgan Stanley, IBM, NOKIA, Samsung, Google, Coca-Cola, Dell, and eBay.

Principle 6: The Tyranny of Consensus—Why Design-by-Democracy Kills Great Marketing

We touched on this in previous chapters, but this concept can't be emphasized enough. Committees don't build iconic brands; they bury them. The business world is riddled with a peculiar pathology: the delusion that marketing decisions, from logos to taglines to campaigns, should be subjected to a gauntlet of opinions from every department, spouse, and bored board member with a Wi-Fi connection. Picture this: Months evaporate as teams debate fonts like theologians parsing scripture. "We need buy-in!" becomes a rallying cry, masking fear of accountability. Suzy in accounting, whose branding expertise begins and ends with admiring GEICO's gecko commercials, frets over fonts. Steve in IT, fresh off his junior-year marketing elective, demands a "warmer yellow." Meanwhile, the CEO's wife lobbies for Comic Sans because it "just feels better." "Feels better" to whom? Stop doing this. Imagine applying this lunacy elsewhere, such as polling the sales team on depreciation schedules, letting Bobby in logistics vet your outside legal counsel, or allowing your dermatologist's *Grey's Anatomy*-binging assistant to diagnose a mole on your neck. No one puts up with that! Yet in marketing, we tolerate this farce, mistaking democracy for wisdom. The result is mediocrity, served lukewarm on a plate of meh. There's a cost to everything and mediocrity is the cost of marketing inclusivity.

Consensus-driven branding is both inefficient and dangerous. It elevates uninformed opinions ("I think...") to the weight of expertise. Your agency spends years mastering color theory, consumer psychology, and cultural nuance, only to be overruled by someone whose creative pinnacle is a PowerPoint template. Steve Jobs didn't crowdsource the iPhone's design. Jeff Bezos didn't take a poll on whether humans would buy toilet paper online. They believed in their vision, and implemented and adjusted along the way. There's no substitute for steady expertise and experience.

Great marketing demands courage, not committees. It requires leaders who say:

- No, we won't test our tagline on interns and second cousins.
- No, 20-year-olds aren't doing our social media strategy because they "understand" Instagram.
- No, your friend's Pinterest board isn't a brand strategy.
- No, we won't dilute bold ideas to placate the lowest common denominator.

An important part of humility that we talked about earlier is not letting amateurs vote on your work. I've spent decades learning to distrust my own biases. My job isn't to "like" a campaign; it is to fight for what's effective. That means ignoring Larry in accounting's font preferences and the board member's daughter who "dabbles in Canva."

You can build a brand that blends into the beige wallpaper of corporate safe bets. Or you can bet on talent, those rare minds who see beyond focus groups and fear. History doesn't remember committees. It remembers icons that brought bold ideas to life.

Ask yourself these questions when approaching a campaign or creative project:

- Is it appropriate?
- Why do I feel this way about our approach? Does it matter how I feel?
- How will our customers feel? How do we want them to feel?
- What is it about me that's making me react to this design or strategy, good or bad?

Being skeptical and humble about your role will help you come to an appropriate and better design sooner, and likely more efficiently and economically. Let the experts guide you, and be guided by skepticism. Don't waste your time on people who are not experts.

THE CREATIVE REVIEW — TOM FISH BURNE

We love it! Just one edit... | Let's make it even stronger. | Our VP has some notes.

Can we see the other concept? | Let's try merging them. | Perfect! Now let's test it. | Sorry, we'll have to start over.

Principle 7: Time

Many people throw around marketing as if it's a project. "Let's build a brand!" Poof, like magic, a month after a logo, product definition, sales presentation, and website are developed, your brand is vibrant, recognized, and tearing up the competition. Of course, this is laughable but sadly thought to be true in many quarters. Brands require time to develop good creative or anything worthwhile in marketing. For campaigns to be effective, time-in-market is an inescapable and crucial gravitational law. For mature brands to stay relevant, their concept of time is different than a startup who is rolling out a new product. Since business lifecycles are different in these examples, strategies and resources allocated to each ought to reflect business goals, which will dictate campaign strategies. Today, access to digital media can shorten the time it takes for some brands to achieve their goals, but they still require customers to experience them and develop those feelings we talked about earlier. Certainly, digital media can also shorten the time for brands to reach people, but reach and brand experience are not inseparable; they're forever married.

Though time is a crucial element in marketing/branding alchemy, it is also relative. Time to market can be shorter for recognizable brands because they already have a footprint. If Procter & Gamble wants to introduce a new product, it's likely to find space on supermarket shelves and digital shelves rather quickly because it's got the money and juice to make it happen. For lesser-known brands who may not have P&G's girth, contacts, and distribution capabilities, it's a more challenging, though not impossible, road. That means it requires more time for smaller brands to take a foothold in the marketplace.

It may have been easier for Ford to become a household name when the company first started with limited competition and only a few enthusiastic buyers at the time. As Ford made the Model T a global a phenomenon of the day with sales in the U.S., Canada, and Great Britain, its brand equity grew quickly. Ford greased the wheels (pun intended) for the entire car market by introducing the automobile to the masses. Oldsmobile, Dodge, Cadillac, and Chrysler were born and followed a relatively similar path. In the 1970s and '80s, Ford's brand faced serious headwinds as quality became an issue, and sales and its brand reputation plummeted among fierce competition from domestic and Japanese imports in a more mature market. Only after it acknowledged and recognized the company was suffering from quality issues did they refocus on quality initiative. "Quality is Job 1" became the tagline that spoke to employees first to let them know quality products drive business success. That campaign lasted 17 years. The Job 1 campaign appealed to consumers and investors to woo them back after they abandoned the brand because the brand abandoned them. Only after the quality issues were addressed did the market regain confidence in Ford, and not a moment before that, albeit reluctantly at first. Some would argue the company has never fully recovered from its quality issues, even today.

Campaign consistency and longevity signal to the market that brands are here to stay. Large brands usually don't pull campaigns after six months because "it's not working" or "we don't have enough traffic to our website." Allstate didn't halt "Mayhem" after two years because some executive felt like "people were getting tired of it." Successful brands understand the need to constantly remind the market of their value over longer periods of time. Long-term campaigns deliver the value of familiarity and serve as constant reminders, a drumbeat of the brand's value. Everyone recognizes Flo from Progressive Insurance because her campaign started in 2008 and is still going strong. The GEICO gecko first appeared in 1999. The Marlboro Man campaign started in 1954 and ended in 1999. United Airlines' Fly the Friendly Skies was revived in 2013 after it was benched in 1999 and ran for about a decade. Capital One's What's in Your Wallet? advertising campaign began in 2000 and continues through today. Time. Time. Time.

Principle 8: Dispatch FOMO

We need to replace FOMO with a strategic approach to trends and technology because the cost is extraordinarily high. Fear of missing out (FOMO) isn't just a buzzword; it's a serious costly addiction. Every LinkedIn guru, TikTok influencer, and self-proclaimed "visionary" peddles the next big thing. Trends explode overnight, fueled by hype and desperation. Not every trend deserves your attention or your budget.

Before surrendering to FOMO, pause and interrogate the trend:

1. Is this relevant to our brand and audience?
2. Will it align with your core values, or is it just noise?
3. Do we have the resources to execute it well? Trends demand speed, but half-baked efforts waste time and trust.
4. What's the realistic ROI? Viral fame is fleeting. Can this trend drive *lasting* value? Does it fit in our branding strategy? What is the visibility?

Take Clubhouse's meteoric rise and spectacular flameout. When Clubhouse burst onto the scene in 2020, it was hailed as revolutionary. The audio-only app lured millions—even Elon Musk and Oprah made appearances—and it sparked clones like Twitter Spaces. Clients clamored, "We need a Clubhouse strategy NOW!" Our response? Wait. Observe. Breathe. We asked clients, "Are you ready to build an audience on a new platform dependent on migrating huge networks from existing platforms? Is fragmenting your efforts across another unproven channel worth it currently? What is our long-term objective here?" Before we knew it, Clubhouse's novelty faded. Competition, user fatigue, and monetization struggles gutted its relevance. By resisting the frenzy, our clients saved six-figure budgets and avoided chasing ghosts.

QR codes made their debut in 2003 but languished for years. Early adoption in the U.S. was dismal because users hated clunky apps and tedious steps. Clients demanded QR codes on billboards, despite the absurdity: "Drivers will scan them at 70 mph!" We pushed back, even losing a client (who later happily returned). But COVID changed everything QR code–related. Smartphones integrated QR readers into cameras while contactless needs skyrocketed. Restaurants, retailers, and events embraced QR codes for menus, payments, and safety. QR codes moved from a trend a decade earlier to becoming ubiquitous because they solved real problems. We adapted swiftly, leveraging their newfound utility while avoiding earlier pitfalls.

Choosing strategy over hysteria is hard. But we know FOMO is a liar. Clubhouse promised revolution but delivered a fad. QR codes flopped until context made them essential. Adapt when facts and relevance are on your side, pivot when utility aligns with purpose, and always be guided by your principles.

7 The Triangle Offense: Frequency, Reach, and Creative

The triangle offense in basketball was popularized by Hall of Fame Chicago Bulls and Los Angeles Lakers Head Coach Phil Jackson and his assistant coach Tex Winter, who originally developed the system. The system involved three players in key positions on the court and emphasized movement and spacing. The triangle offense has been praised for its effectiveness, but it is also complex and requires players with high basketball IQs who can make quick decisions. It brought Jackson and Winters multiple NBA Championships during their runs with the Bulls in the 1990s and Lakers in the 2000s.

Marketing's triangle offense is frequency, reach, and creative in the way it strategically balances multiple elements to achieve success. Just as the triangle offense relies on precise spacing, continuous movement, and flexible decision-making to create scoring opportunities, an effective marketing campaign uses a similar approach to deliver results. Frequency (how often a message is seen), reach (where and how many people see it), and creative (the content and design of the message) must work together to deliver success. Similarly, in marketing and

advertising in particular, balancing frequency and reach with compelling creative ensures that the message is delivered often enough to be effective, to a broad enough audience to be impactful, and in a way that resonates with consumers. Both the triangle offense and marketing strategy require careful coordination and an understanding of timing, audience, and execution to be truly effective.

It's important to consider certain elements of frequency, reach, and creative depending on the platform. For example, reach via digital can be somewhat of a black hole because search or social algorithms are somewhat of a black hole, contributing to waste. So, it's reach quality that matters most, and that's subjective because creative is a momentary element that can catch fire, connect to culture, or land on deaf ears.

Assuming you've got the right audience and channel, this troika is vital to campaign design. While some argue this concept is outdated, I disagree and am willing to debate the issue. Let's make this simple: in an era of fragmented media and minuscule attention spans, imagine running a TV commercial with great creative only three times a week during a popular show (frequency), sending only one email to a global database (reach), or missing on social media campaigns because creative doesn't connect but expect results. We live in a multi-screen, multi-channel world where businesses are competing in an attention-based economy. Frequency, reach, and creative are fundamental principles that give campaigns a chance to be effective.

There are no set formulas replicable over time and audiences; anyone who tells you differently is either inexperienced or lying. Full stop. Reach and creative aren't necessarily equally weighted in every campaign. One could argue you can have terrible creative concepts but still can have an effective campaign with the right frequency and reach. However, that same campaign is highly likely to fail if its frequency and reach are off target.

The troika doesn't work if budgets and resources aren't available to fuel campaigns. Assuming budgets are adequate, our first approach is making sure we have the most engaging creative possible, precisely targeted for reach, and ensure we touch our audience enough for them get the message. Sometimes reality hits us in between the eyes and budgets aren't adequate. If you find yourself in that situation, choose quality over quantity, perhaps smaller, more focused campaigns. Whatever it is, ensure the highest quality creative as possible to best represent your brand.

On Frequency

How many times do people need to see you and experience your message for you to achieve your goals or for people to act? Industry pros claim it's five to seven times for people to recognize your brand. Believe it or not, that range was coined in the 1930s, way before Don Draper came on the scene, and it's still being referenced. I honestly don't know how many times people need to see your message today, but because it's not the 1930s and we're inundated with brand messages on more devices and channels, my take is that frequency number is much higher.

Frequency is the number of times a person will be exposed to your ad or message. Your reach will highly depend on your budget and resources as well as your target audience. But how many times does it take to convince someone to buy your stuff, service, or ideas? There are many factors that determine how many times someone needs to see your message to convert them to a buyer. Is your product new? Is it a "me too"? What's the consumer motivation? Did you launch a product and two weeks later a natural disaster happened? If you're selling toilet paper to a price-sensitive audience, then a promotional "30 percent off" message may be a motivator, and as a result, it may require less frequency. If you're Samsung and trying to win business from Apple customers, your frequency may need to be much higher, along with an impactful message to get Apple customers to feel better about both leaving Apple and Samsung's brand. The lifecycle of the business or campaign can also influence frequency. If McDonald's is selling a Big Mac, it may need less frequency because both McDonald's and Big Macs are widely recognized brands. People know Mickey D's; they trust and even prefer the brand. Though, if McDonald's is facing a drop in Big Mac sales, it may need to lean into cool creative and frequency. Now, if you're a new fast-food chain, you'll need to tell people who you are, share your delicious menu items, and encourage them to try your stuff, all while creating a feeling for why customers will love your food. No easy task. In this case, your campaign requires more customer touches to generate awareness, trust, curiosity, interest, and action at the same time.

In basketball terms, think of frequency like the number of times Michael Jordan gets the ball. The more touches he gets, the more chances he has to score.

On Reach and Deep Reach

Reach is about the number of people who are exposed to a marketing message at any given time. High-reach campaigns allow you to reach as many people as possible, and low-reach campaigns target either less people or more specific audiences. As I mentioned earlier, while reach has always been tricky, today it's more elusive than ever. With the advent of digital, reach can be out of reach. For business pages, Facebook's organic rules limit reach, data shows programmatic digital advertising is an incredible source of waste, and people are cutting the chord on TV, limiting the reach of cable subscribers. Audiences are fragmented across streaming audio platforms, like Spotify and Apple Music. So how exactly do you reach customers effectively? How do we think about reach to help us achieve our marketing goals? If your goal is to generate high levels of brand awareness, reach for deep reach! Deep reach is meeting your audience where they are, be it connecting through culture like sports and music, engaging key opinion leaders (KOLs) and influencers, or finding events that bring people together. Deep reach is finding relevancy more than about the number of people reached. Obviously, the more relevant, the better.

Who are your customers? Where are they? What is important to them? Reach is a vital tool to deliver your message to allow you to communicate, teach, and develop relationships with your customers. For example, you're a hospital system that just acquired a competitor and are looking to deliver more services in your new market. You know you have an existing patient base to reach, but you'll need to grow your reach outside of your existing patient base to continue to grow. You'll need to solve for the following: Where do patients come from and for what service? If analysis shows patients mostly come from referring physicians, then referring physicians are your target market and you can construct your marketing strategy and priorities from that cornerstone. This helps avoid costly marketing mistakes, in this case running full speed into patient marketing. By the way, this is another example of a uniquely American situation.

Reach allows us to meet the people we want to engage with our products and services where they're at, preferably in a place that's desirable and comfortable for them. This concept holds true across platforms including TV or billboards, email or direct mail, sales meetings and social media. The "where" could be the Food Channel or a mom blog, a client dinner or a TikTok ad. It doesn't matter where that place is; what matters is that it is relevant and there are enough of the people you're trying to reach to make it worth your time. Where creative may be subjective, reach can be fickle. You can reach your customers, but have you made an impact? I've always been an advocate for deep, meaningful reach.

Deep reach connects your brand with a smaller, more targeted audience in a highly impactful and meaningful way, rather than trying to reach the broadest audience possible. This approach focuses on engaging a specific group of consumers who are more likely to be interested in the product or service, and it often involves personalized messaging, content, and experiences that resonate deeply with this audience.

Deep reach can land higher engagement and conversion rates. By focusing on a more defined audience, perhaps smaller or maybe not, marketers can create messages that are more relevant and appealing, which

> **"Marketing is not the art of finding clever ways to dispose of what you make. It is the art of creating genuine relevance and value for customers."**
>
> —Philip Kotler, "Father of Modern Marketing," in *Marketing 4.0: Moving from Traditional to Digital* (2016)

leads to higher engagement and better conversion rates. For example, a brand targeting eco-conscious consumers might craft highly specific campaigns around sustainability, leading to more meaningful interactions and brand loyalty within that niche. Deep reach allows marketers to better allocate resources for more efficiency. Instead of spreading budgets across a broad audience with varying levels of interest, deep reach concentrates efforts on those most likely to convert, maximizing ROI. Because the emphasis is on quality over quantity, it builds stronger brand relationships and fosters deeper emotional connections with their audience. This can lead to increased customer loyalty and advocacy, as consumers feel more understood and valued by the brand. In a rapidly changing market, where consumer preferences can shift quickly, deep reach allows brands to be more agile. By closely understanding a niche audience, marketers can more effectively anticipate and respond to changes in consumer behavior, ensuring that their messaging stays relevant.

And once you find audience relevancy through deep reach, give them a reason to respond—scarcity, discounting, urgency, whatever you can do to nudge and motivate your audience to act. If you're selling jackets at the end of the season and you're a discounter, how do you turn stagnant inventory into revenue without diluting your brand? The key lies in strategic message frequency, a tactic that transforms urgency into action. Deep reach isn't about shouting louder; it's about shouting smarter to the right audience. Start by zeroing in on your "discount cluster," the bargain hunters who've bought sale items before or browsed clearance pages. Unlike refrigerator shoppers, discount hunters thrive on urgency and value, so craft a drumbeat of messages across their preferred channels. Escalate emails from "40% Off" to "Final Hours! Prices Slashed!" Deploy SMS blasts for flash sales, and retarget cart abandoners with real-time inventory alerts like "3 left at this price!" By layering scarcity ("Only 8 jackets left!") and social proof ("200 bought today!"), you tap into psychological triggers that push indecisive buyers to act. But restraint is critical: cap emails to three a week (spiking to daily in the final days) and limit ads to three a day to avoid fatigue. When frequency aligns with audience intent and timing, it's not noise. It's a precision tool that turns clearance sales into loyal customers. Like frequency, deep reach's strings are pulled by your budget. The more budget, the more your message can get around. For those organic social fans who are scoffing at this because of viral something something, enjoy your hopeium and good luck staring at your screen. Okay, next topic.

On Creative

Creativity is the flashy third principle that deserves the spotlight. Let's get one thing straight: creativity isn't the third leg of the marketing stool; it's the fuel that makes the Ferrari go. Sure, strategy and data matter, but without creativity, your chances of going far are slim. So, what is marketing creativity and why does it matter? If you Google creativity, you'll drown in six billion definitions. Is it Wendy's roasting trolls on Twitter? Is it Crazy Eddie screaming about "INSANE" prices until he actually went insane? Or is it Bed Bath & Beyond's coupons haunting your mailbox like a persistent ghost from 2003? I'll spare you the existential crisis. Creativity boils down to two things:

1. How you scream into the void (a.k.a. messaging).
2. How you turn customers into cult members (a.k.a. the brand mythmaking we talked about earlier).

Let's start with the first, because *everyone* loves a good show. Ever gotten a piece of mail from American Express? It's like receiving a wedding invitation from the Queen of England. The paper feels like it was woven by silkworms getting a massage at a day spa. The fonts and the aesthetic? So clean you can eat off them. That's creativity. Now, compare that to your local bank's direct mail. You know, the one that looks like it was designed by Uncle Jimmy in his garage after three beers. You don't feel guilty tossing it; you feel relieved. So, the lesson here is creativity doesn't require a Fortune 500 budget. It requires not letting Uncle Jimmy out of his garage.

While we're in creative, let's talk mascots. The GEICO gecko isn't just a lizard; he's become a cultural icon. Without GEICO's ad budget to power advertising placement? He'd just be another reptile begging for crickets on the side of the road. Creativity without reach and the budget to power it is like a stand-up comedian performing to an empty room. Tragic.

Creativity isn't about being cool. It's about being unignorable and captivating. Good creativity? AT&T's Lily hypnotizing us into upgrading our data plans or switching to AT&T. Bad creativity: the latest TikTok unboxing video by 5,000 companies. Creativity should be at every touchpoint, from emails to billboards to customer service calls. All should feel like chapters in the same ridiculously addictive novel.

If your creativity isn't making someone say, "Wait, did they really just do that?" you're doing it wrong. At its core, meaningful creative helps you better tell your story and connect with your audience. Exceptional creative connects on a different level: emotionally. But again, that process takes courage.

Tap into people's emotions to connect them to your business and brand, to inspire how you'd like customers to feel about you. Here's a list of thirty emotions that you can use to create campaigns that connect:

- Happiness
- Sadness
- Anger
- Fear
- Surprise
- Disgust
- Love
- Joy
- Excitement
- Contentment
- Anxiety
- Guilt
- Shame
- Jealousy
- Envy

- Pride
- Hope
- Relief
- Curiosity
- Surprise
- Frustration
- Embarrassment
- Empathy
- Compassion
- Gratitude
- Awe
- Trust
- Anticipation
- Loneliness
- Regret

When you look at the emotions, remember campaigns that resonated not just with you but in our culture.

Emotions come alive through storytelling, music, touch, images, or a combination of sensory experiences. Keep in mind the human brain processes images 60,000 times faster than text, which is why social media, television, and video are so powerful. It's also why pharmaceutical advertisers show happy people with lots of movement and activity. Our eyes buy in first, and so bowling, riding bikes, playing softball, and sailing help mask the voiceover where they are telling us that their drugs can cause hideous side effects, adverse health conditions, and even death. But hey, "ask your doctor."

It's hyperbole to say we now live in a world where all creative should be designed for multiple platforms. Of course it should. TV commercials should be on YouTube and social, email campaigns should be connected to social, billboard ads should double as social posts, and so on. Assuming deep reach, your message is now in front of relevant audiences across different channels and platforms, thereby increasing the chances of your message being delivered to your audience. In whatever you do, prioritizing emotions with your creative approach is always a good idea because if you hit the right note, you'll bypass the thinking mechanism upstairs and go straight to their hearts, where their wallet resides. Don't be afraid to shun or ignore what your competitors are doing and embrace creativity to develop a unique personality for your brand.

Creativity is tricky and takes courage. After all, there's a price to pay for originality. Spectacular success and failure could be two sides of the same coin. And yet, while there's no single agreed-upon definition of creativity, many studies show that it can indeed pay off. One *Harvard Business Review* advertising study by Werner J. Reinartz and Peter Saffert revealed, "A euro invested in a highly creative ad campaign had nearly double the sales impact of a euro spent on a noncreative campaign."[40]

Now let's talk about creativity in customer engagement and its role in brand mythmaking. In 2016, Pokémon took its already iconic brand into the stratosphere when it introduced Pokémon Go. The game created unique and immersive player experiences that revolutionized the gaming industry. Pokémon Go blended the digital and physical realms, allowing players to experience the virtual Pokémon world within their own real-world environment. This blending of realities was so popular, and people were so focused on the game, that they put themselves in dangerous situations, causing mayhem, accidents, even death. According to "Death by Pokémon Go: The Economic and Human Cost of Using Apps While Driving" a study by Mara Faccio and John J. McConnell of Purdue University, Pokémon Go was responsible for a "disproportionate increase" in collisions near PokéStops in Tippecanoe County, Indiana, which is where the study was conducted. "The game was introduced on July 6, 2016," Faccio and McConnell wrote. "Within one month, worldwide, the game was downloaded more than 100 million times." The study went on to conclude that county-wide the app resulted in car damage, injuries, and fatalities costing $5.2 million. Nationwide, the study estimated mind-boggling costs that ranged between $2 billion to $7.3 billion.[41] Pokémon Go kept players engaged, and some were dangerously hooked, through continuous updates, new features, and new Pokémon releases. The game successfully encouraged players to explore their surroundings, connect with others, and actively participate in the Pokémon world, creating a truly immersive and engaging experience.

> **"Creativity is the currency of modern marketing. It's not about shouting louder—it's about speaking to the heart in a way algorithms can't replicate."**
>
> —Arianna Huffington, Thrive Global Summit (2021)

Let's examine another example of engagement creativity from Starbucks. In 2014, the coffee juggernaut launched its White Cup Contest, a social media campaign that encouraged customers to showcase their creativity by doodling on their white Starbucks cups, taking a photo of it, and sharing their designs on social platforms using the hashtag #WhiteCupContest. The announcement invited customers to "imagine a Starbucks iconic white cup covered in pink hearts, colorful zig zag lines, or an artistic sweep of shapes encircling the green Siren logo."

This campaign captured the imagination of customers and immersed them in co-creating content. The user-generated content put customers in the center of the campaign, allowing them to create art and tell stories about Starbucks on their own social media platforms, extending Starbuck's reach. The winning design by Brita Lynn Thompson, a Pittsburgh art student at the time, was subsequently printed on a limited-edition reusable cup, thus giving longevity to the campaign.

For good measure, let's look at one more creative campaign that engaged customers: how the iconic Coca-Cola got people to "Share a Coke." In 2011, Coke wanted to create a sense of personal connection to its products and encourage consumers to share their special Coca-Cola moments by personalizing Coke bottles and cans, replacing the brand's logo with popular names and phrases.

Consumers were invited to find bottles or cans with their names and names of friends and family members and post their experiences on social media via the hashtag #ShareACoke. The campaign achieved an astonishing hit almost instantly and generated widespread social media buzz. The hashtag #ShareACoke went viral, with millions of mentions across various social platforms of people sharing photos and stories of their own name on a bottle or can of Coke. Coke tapped into our visceral desire to hear and see our own name, making people feel special and more connected to the brand. It gave control of its brand to its customers, allowing them to leverage their own people network on social media and creativity to create a sense of individuality and community at the same time. The campaign was credited with increasing sales and brand loyalty.

In the previous examples, brands gave up control over their creative and allowed customers to run with it, but in all cases, these campaigns were carefully implemented and well thought-out. The success of all three campaigns can be attributed to being well-defined, and to some extent, the brands creating a playpen for customers to create and engage.

This kind of creativity can be tricky. For example, user-generated creative campaigns can be hijacked if not designed thoughtfully. Take, for example, the 2012 McDStories campaign by McDonald's, which encourage customers to share positive experiences and stories on Twitter via the hashtag #McDStories. That campaign quickly went where McDonald's did not want it to go. Twitter users, customers or not, hijacked the hashtag and took the opportunity to share negative experiences at McDonald's. The hashtag became a nightmare for McDonald's as customers vented their frustration with food quality and shared negative stories about their experience with the brand.

Creativity isn't just for consumer brands. B2B brands can benefit from an injection of creative juices. A 2022 study by LinkedIn entitled "Building a Memorable B2B Brand: Who Will Be the Next Iconic Brand?"[42] found the following:

- About 80 percent of B2B marketing budgets are spent on lead generation or performance marketing.
- B2B buyers value memorable creative that drives emotional connection as much as their B2C counterparts.
- On a 1–5 scale of creative effectiveness, with 5 marking the most impactful creative, 71 percent of B2B ads score 1, and 71 percent of B2B Ads are likely to generate no sales.

- Creative is the biggest factor contributing to sales in an ad campaign (47 percent). Great creative generates 10 to 20 times more sales.
- Brands with more emotional appeal have 198 times more followers on LinkedIn than those less creative.
- The average B2B company tends to have lower creative scores, despite the market saying it needs creativity.

And why not? Aren't B2B buyers human? Of course they are, and that's precisely why B2B business should consider moving out of their comfort zone to create more creative ads. If there are customers on the other side, isn't it better to do whatever it takes to connect with them? Great creative then becomes just as important to brand building and as important to driving long-term revenue growth in B2B as it is in consumer marketing.

How Do We Know Good Creative?

Creative is ultimately subjective. However, there are a certain concoction of elements that I look for to help me judge creativity. These include three key areas:

1. Originality and innovation in message and visuals.
2. Messaging that connects to culture, tapping into consumer psyche.
3. Relevancy to customers or the audience.

In practice, frequency, reach, and creative elements should work synergistically to maximize the impact of a campaign: reach ensures that the message is seen by the right audience, frequency reinforces the message to make it stick, and creative ensures that the message is effective and memorable.

Keep in mind, however, there are limitations to this approach. High frequency without thoughtful creative can lead to ad fatigue, where the audience becomes annoyed or desensitized to the message, diminishing its effectiveness. Over-emphasis on reach might result in a campaign that spreads too thin, reaching many people but not effectively engaging any particular segment. Additionally, even the best creative content can fall flat if it isn't supported by sufficient reach and frequency.

The Audacity of Creativity: Why Safe Marketing Is the Riskiest Choice

Not all creative campaigns are created equal, but mediocrity always costs the same. In a world drowning in lookalike ads and me-too messaging, "safe" creativity isn't cautious; it's a recipe for mind-numbing failure. Yet businesses keep cloning competitors, mistaking mimicry for strategy. Why? Because it's easier to justify failure when everyone else is failing the same way. But true creativity isn't about comfort. It's about courage, and courage seems to be fleeting these days. Range Rover's Plugin Hybrid campaign didn't show soccer moms idling in school drop-off lines or pulling up to the mall parking lot, which is literally how Range Rovers are used. Instead, it scaled the Great Wall of China's 999-step incline, a feat no customer will ever attempt. Why? Because logic doesn't sell luxury. Emotion does. By trading minivans for mountains, Range Rover didn't just avoid the sea of sameness, it drowned competitors in a tidal wave of adrenaline. Range Rover knows boring brands die quietly. Bold ones rewrite the rules, and that's what they did. AFLAC's duck brought the campaign from absurdity to iconic. Imagine pitching "Our spokesperson is a duck." AFLAC's team didn't just say yes; they bet the farm on a mascot that mocked the industry's stuffiness. The result produced a cultural icon that spawned imitators like LiMu emu and GEICO's gecko and turned a commodity into a memorable and beloved character. These campaigns worked well because they were powered by creativity and budget.

For several years, the Antonellis, a real-life cheese shop couple, became the face of a 2-percent cashback card. Their charm wasn't an accident. Capital One blanketed screens with their folksy appeal, marrying relatability with relentless frequency. The takeaway? Creativity without reach is a tree falling in an empty forest, while reach without budget is fantasy.

For you Gen X readers in the United States, remember the iconic Toys R Us "I Don't Want to Grow Up" song and McDonald's "Big Mac" chant aren't just jingles; they're generational imprints. Decades later, they're etched into our brains, proving creativity's true power: outliving mediums and channels.

Creativity isn't confined to campaigns. It's the Golden State Warriors raining three-pointers, the New England Patriots' aura of invincibility, or

the Arkansas Razorbacks' "40 Minutes of Hell" on the basketball court that sent shivers through opponents even before the game started. These teams weaponized identity. Your brand is the sum of every customer touchpoint and experience, but safety is not your friend. Safe creativity is an oxymoron. Range Rover's SUV will never climb the Great Wall. No one buys insurance from a duck. Cheese makers don't sell credit cards. Yet these campaigns work because they dare to disconnect from reality. They trade logic for magic, comfort for memorability. Ask yourself:

- What's your "Dragon Challenge"? What audacious idea could redefine your category?
- Are you the duck or the agent? Will you disrupt or disappear?
- Will consistency outlive your campaign? GEICO's gecko didn't win in a day, a month, or a year. Neither will you.

The choice is clear: risk being remarkable, or guarantee being forgotten.

The Shortsightedness of Short-termism

Let's continue exploring the impact of short-termism on marketing. Perhaps more than any other time in the history of human commerce, businesses are demanding short-term results more often. Spurred by quarter-to-quarter performance, the unquenchable thirst for KPIs and "analytics," the demand for immediate results is both seemingly overwhelming and boring. Demand generation and conversion command an outsized share of marketing's culture. In some cases, quarter-to-quarter management is being pushed to month to month, exacting more pressure on marketers and businesses than ever, as if businesses are day-trading stations. But time and again, effective marketing relies on the most precious element in our human existence: time. Time is key to brand equity and building your business. Time requires another fading element: patience. "Time is a friend of wonderful companies and the enemy of mediocre ones," said Warren Buffet.

Let's explore some wonderful companies who use time to unlock value in marketing. UPS's iconic campaigns were specifically designed to get a message to multiple audiences. Created by Ogilvy, the We Love Logistics campaign illustrated UPS's commitment to delivering transportation and supply chain solutions that power its customers' businesses. The five-year campaign began in 2010 and ended in 2015. And who can forget Dos Equis's The Most Interesting Man in the World. That campaign kicked off in 2006 and ended in 2016. All-State's Mayhem commercials, which started in 2010, are still going strong as I write in early 2025. All three of these unforgettable campaigns, as with other campaigns that have made their mark on our culture as well as on the bottom line, have two curial elements working together: time and campaign consistency.

Time and campaign consistency tell your customers you're here to stay. UPS didn't pull the campaign after six months because "We need to strengthen on our balance sheet, so we're pulling advertising for this quarter." Successful brands understand they need to constantly remind their existing customers of their value and at the same time bring in new customers. Long-term campaigns serve as constant reminders, a drumbeat of the brand's value. Like early grade school students take to repetition, so do people. As humans, we find some comfort in consistency: going to the same restaurants, flying the same airlines, and even connecting and engaging with certain advertising whether on TV or online.

More on Creativity, Because We Need More Nuance Here...

In our attention economy, the ability to capture and persuade as quickly as possible stands as one of the most valuable skills. Remember, marketing is about behavior modification, so persuasion in marketing campaigns is not merely about convincing customers to buy your product, service, or ideas; it's about creating a connection, building trust, and driving behavior that leads to long-term success. Let's delve into why persuasion is so vital in marketing and explore some compelling examples of persuasive campaigns that have left a lasting impact.

Isn't persuasion the beating heart of all marketing? At its core, marketing exists to sway audiences, to make your brand's voice louder, brighter, and more irresistible than the competition's. But persuasion isn't always about crafting the perfect slogan or a viral hook. Often, it's the relentless repetition of your message in the right places that wears down resistance and builds unconscious loyalty.

> **"If you would persuade, you must appeal to interest rather than intellect."**
>
> —Benjamin Franklin

Think of it this way: even a mediocre ad, seen 20 times, can out-persuade a brilliant ad seen once. Why? Familiarity breeds trust. Strategic placement (think billboards on busy roads, targeted social feeds, or email inboxes) ensures your brand becomes a background rhythm in your audience's daily life. Over time, this consistency transforms indifference into action: a purchase, a subscription, a share. But true persuasion goes deeper. It's about aligning your message with your audience's unspoken cravings and fears. Are you selling security? Status? Belonging? The best campaigns don't just say, "Buy this." They whisper, "This is who you could be." For example, a budget hotel chain doesn't just advertise "cheap rooms." It sells "adventure without debt" to backpackers or "guilt-free family trips" to parents. By reframing a "low cost" product as a gateway to freedom, it taps into emotions that price tags alone can't reach.

In the end, persuasion isn't manipulation. It simply moves empathy to the forefront. It's understanding your audience so deeply that choosing your brand feels less like a decision and more like destiny.

Good creative requires time. Time to think and play around with ideas, get things wrong, make mistakes, but ultimately develop an approach that connects with your audience. Here's the paradox: bad creative can still work, but only under specific conditions. Take those cringeworthy car dealership commercials plastered with shouting salesmen and flashing text. You might groan, but you remember them. Why? Because while the creative quality is undeniably low, its relentless frequency and consistency drill the message into your brain. The ad isn't necessarily good, but it is unavoidable.

Seen enough times, bad creative can be viewed as a novelty, even funny, which can strike a positive chord with audiences. Hell, I had a tampon commercial stuck in my head from junior year in high school until sophomore year in college! *"OB, it's the way it should be. Just try OB and you'll see!"* Bad creative can survive and even thrive if it's given enough oxygen of frequency. Frequency breathes life into bad creative, which can make bad creative grow on people and even make it loveable.

Bad creative comes in many forms. Let's look at Pepsi's Kendall Jenner campaign. Pepsi clearly missed the mark, even though Pepsi's in-house talent and agency partners are top notch. I don't know who thought trivializing social justice issues and using imagery reminiscent of Black Lives Matter protests was a good idea, but that creative plate of hummus went bad quickly. Bloomingdale's swung and missed badly with its 2015 in-catalogue ad Spike Your Best Friend's Egg Nog, encouraging readers to slip alcohol in their friends' drinks without their knowledge. The ad was broadly condemned for promoting date rape culture and was quickly pulled from the catalog. Again, Bloomingdale's is not short on talent or budget, but these things do happen. These weren't just misfires; they were completely avoidable, self-inflicted mistakes.

I'm not giving a free pass for mediocrity. But the reality is bad creative might succeed despite itself, not because of it. Truly great campaigns, like Apple's minimalist elegance or Nike's motivational storytelling, combine creativity with strategic repetition to forge deeper, more meaningful connections. All of that is naturally powered by money.

In my experience, frequency can salvage bad creative, but it's a shaky lifeline. Brilliant creative + smart media placement + powered by budget = unstoppable persuasion. Aim for creative excellence but never underestimate the raw power of showing up repeatedly.

What Actually Makes "Good Creative" Good?

Good creative is your workhorse. It resonates, provokes, and, above all, works. After decades of watching campaigns soar or flop, I've distilled its essence to three non-negotiables: emotional storytelling, humor, and meaning. Forget "authenticity." Before customers can want your stuff, they want to experience your brand and feel something.

Take emotional storytelling. The best campaigns that we all connect with don't just sell; they stir. Always' Like a Girl campaign didn't peddle menstrual products; it galvanized vulnerability to shatter gender stereotypes and "period shame." It turned a phrase soaked in playground insults into a battle cry for empowerment. That's persuasion masquerading as purpose.

Then there's humor, the great equalizer. Old Spice's "The Man Your Man Could Smell Like" commercial didn't peddle deodorized armpits; it roasted toxic masculinity with surreal absurdity and a wink and a smile. Horses galloping on beaches? Tornadoes of body wash? It worked because it mocked the very idea of "manliness" while selling the very thing it's mocking.

People will resonate with your campaign when it connects with them and if your products or services have meaning to them at the same time. Let's face it, Whole Foods could start hawking gas station sushi tomorrow, and loyalists would call it "disruptive gastronomy." Why? Because they may search for anything to defend the brand they love, the brand they're connected to. Dove's Real Beauty campaign didn't win hearts because it was "authentic." It won because it made women scream, "Finally, someone gets it!" Sometimes, meaning isn't about truth. It's about making your audience feel seen, even if you're selling them soap.

Yeah, bad creative can be unforgettable too. Those local car dealer ads, shouting salesmen, flashing prices, and explosions for no reason are the raccoons of marketing: trashy, but you can't look away. You may say you hate them. But you'll also remember them. Take the OB tampons jingle that haunted my brain from high school to college. Was it good? No. Did it work? Ask my incessant involuntary mental replay, then ask why this is the second time I am mentioning it.

Good creative dies in silence without distribution. Bad creative thrives on relentless repetition. That jingle I mocked? It's colonized my brain for years. That cringey car ad is still playing on a loop in your subconscious. But real creativity isn't confined to ads. It's in the gutsy choices you make offscreen. It could be in picking a physical location for your business, the type of fabric you choose for your products, and so on. In the end, good creative takes time. So make us laugh, cry, or cringe. Make people argue about your ad at Thanksgiving dinner. Because in a world drowning in content, the only thing worse than bad creative is being ignored.

Aristotle in Advertising

I should've paid more attention during the Greek philosophy lessons in high school. I was probably doodling in the margins thinking about the Big East Tournament, blissfully unaware that Aristotle's ethos, pathos, and logos would one day become the holy trinity of selling overpriced sneakers, acidic coffee, and sugar water. Thanks, Aristotle. Your 2,300-year-old insights are now the backbone of convincing people they need a $1,200 phone to feel cool.

But let's not get ahead of ourselves. Aristotle's modes of persuasion, ethos (credibility), pathos (emotional manipulation), and logos (logical sleight-of-hand), are the secret sauce behind every marketing campaign that's ever made you cry into your credit card statement. Let's dive into a few classics, shall we?

Nike's Just Do It, because nothing says "empowerment" like handing over $250 for those shoes. I mean Nike really made people believe that buying their sneakers will transform you into Serena Williams or Michael Jordan. Their Just Do It campaign is a masterclass in emotional extortion (pathos). Put the tagline on a billboard, show someone climbing a mountain at dawn, and suddenly people are somehow convinced their treadmill desk, walk in the park, or hooping with friends qualifies as "pushing boundaries."

Then there's logos! Nike's genius lies in pairing sweat-soaked inspiration with cold, hard logic: "Our shoes have science! Air cushions! Space technology!" And let's not forget ethos, because if Michael Jordan wears these kicks while dunking, sure, they'll help you dunk...on a Nerf hoop. But that brand, that lifestyle and movement, translated into so much more than shoes. Millions of people have been buying polyester shirts with swooshes to "symbolize personal empowerment." Sure, Jan.

Apple's Think Different celebrated rebels, visionaries, but we've now come to know those ads were a masterclass in selling conformity. Because nothing says radical individualism and independence like owning the same white earbuds as 1.5 billion people. Apple's Think Different campaign is the pièce de résistance of ethos. By slapping black-and-white photos of Einstein, Gandhi, and MLK on a screen, Apple whispered, "You too can change the world...by buying this very expensive laptop with the forbidden fruit logo."

The pathos? The audacity to imply that purchasing an iPhone makes you the creative descendant of Galileo or Michaelangelo. "Our products are for innovators!" Cool, cool, though never mind that 90 percent of those "innovators" use them to scroll social media and for selfies. It's persuasion so slick, Aristotle himself would've traded feta for AirPods.

Let's examine Coca-Cola's Share a Coke campaign replacing its logo with names like "Anna" and "George," because nothing fosters human connection like slapping your friend's name on a diabetes-inducing beverage. The pathos here is diabolical: "Look, it's *your name*! You're *special*!" (Spoiler: They only printed the top 100 names. Sorry, "Phil.") The logos? "People love seeing their names!" Sure, if you ignore the fact that it's a psychological trick straight from a used-car salesman's playbook. And the ethos? Coca-Cola, the brand that brought you polar bears sipping soda in the Arctic, convinced you this wasn't a desperate ploy to reverse a decade of declining sales. It worked. Sales jumped 2 percent.

Let's not forget the times when persuasion backfired harder than an influencer's apology video. This is when Aristotle rolled in his grave. Enter Ford's Pinto, a car so poorly named, it's a miracle it didn't come with a parental advisory sticker. In Brazil and Mexico, "pinto" translates to...well, let's just say it's slang for male genitalia. Pinto's brand debacle was a masterclass in cultural tone-deafness, proving that even Aristotle's wisdom can't save you if you name your car after a certain body part. But persuasion isn't always the answer. Sure, Aristotle's troika can work wonders, until it doesn't. Overdo the pathos, and you're the creepy uncle at Christmas: "Buy this collagen cream, or you'll die alone!" Bombard folks with logos, and you're just another spreadsheet-wielding robot. As for ethos? One scandal, and your credibility goes up in flames. Take it from Ford: persuasion without cultural awareness and relevance is like serving a steak at a vegan convention. You might get attention, but it won't be the attention you're looking for.

More on Trends

I put up the caution sign about trends earlier in this book, but let's get into it a bit more. Trends can be both important and dangerous. Hitching your brand to a trend can help your business or product stay relevant in the minds of your customers. Trends can dictate consumer behavior, however momentary. Take Wendy's brand, which has done a great job focusing on social media. The company's strategy is to stay on top of social media trends, especially on Twitter (I still ain't calling it the other thing), where their witty and often humorous interactions have made the brand stand out. Wendy's is intentional about social media trends, it owns that medium, and as a result, it's become an important part of its overall marketing.

Trends allow businesses to capitalize on momentary opportunities ripping through the culture. Some trends hang around for some time while others fade quickly. When live streaming became popular, companies like Amazon and Google capitalized on this trend by introducing their own live-streaming services (Twitch and YouTube Live). Similarly, brands that embraced influencer marketing early on, like Glossier, saw significant growth by leveraging the power of social media influencers to build credibility and reach new audiences. As we discussed earlier, in the case of Clubhouse's trend, it was a miserable failure. Blockbuster video seemed oblivious to a monumental streaming trend, and it cost the company its life.

Our philosophy is we don't chase. That doesn't make it right or wrong; it's just our firm's philosophy. We rarely participate in trends, and when we do, it's only when we believe they align with our clients' business and we see a meaningful, longer horizon where we can hop in and ride them for a bit. We also want to take advantage of any spillover effects that can meaningfully impact other areas of the business, like public relations or key opinion leadership. So, while we may choose not to capitalize on a particular trend, we can study it and comment on it in the press or social media, for example.

Trends can also encourage short-termism. Over-reliance on trends can lead to a short-term focus at the expense of long-term strategy and feed that day-trading mentality. Focusing on trends that fade can leave companies with lots of activity at the expense of productivity, an unwanted distraction. For instance, when brands jumped on the Pokémon Go craze in 2016, many created promotions and content around the game. However, as the game's popularity waned, so did the impact of those marketing efforts, leaving brands scrambling for the next big thing. So, we don't chase because we don't want to waste resources.

A Word About B2B Marketing: From Boring to Breathtaking

B2B marketing is like the kale smoothie of marketing: worthy, nutritious, but about as exciting as a panel discussion on tax policy. Somewhere along the way, businesses decided that professionalism means draining all life, color, and humanity from their messaging. We've been conditioned to believe that decision-makers in suits are immune to emotion, that they only respond to bullet points, jargon, and spreadsheets titled "Circling Back to the Lowest Hanging Fruit in Q3." So, we bombard them with so-called ads that read like robot love letters: "Our cloud-native SaaS solution leverages AI-driven scalability to optimize your mission-critical workflows." Riveting stuff.

The problem isn't that B2B products are complex. The problem is that we've confused clarity with boredom. We've let conservative industry norms, rooted in the fear that creativity might accidentally make the buyer feel something, or draw their attention from features and benefits, stifle campaigns into oblivion. We've also let salespeople lead marketing efforts, and that's a natural mismatch. The sales perspective is about the product, features, and benefits. They need to know products and services inside out, so sell-sheets and presentations in that model follow naturally.

Yet behind every overcrowded sell-sheet is a human. That human is your business buyer.

Take GE Healthcare's Healthcare Reimagined campaign. Instead of harping on "advanced imaging algorithms" and "diagnostic precision," they told stories that made surgeons reach for tissues. One ad followed a child's journey through life-saving surgery, with GE's technology framed not as a cold machine, but as a hero in the narrative. That campaign allowed healthcare professionals to see the product and feel its impact. Suddenly, an MRI scanner wasn't a hunk of metal; it was the reason a kid got to go home. GE brought mythmaking to B2B marketing, and at the time they became the Apple of healthcare—innovative, indispensable, and interesting.

Then there's American Express' Small Business Saturday. In 2010, they could've slapped a generic "We Support Entrepreneurs!" ad in the *Wall Street Journal*. Instead, they turned a post-Thanksgiving Saturday into a national holiday for mom-and-pop shops. They gave small businesses free marketing kits and rallied communities around them. The campaign wasn't about credit card fees or reward points (features and benefits). It was a call to action about belonging and community building. It tapped into the universal truth that everyone roots for the underdog, and that stronger communities are better communities. Billions of dollars later, Small Business Saturday isn't just a campaign; it's widely recognized as a cultural moment of reflection and action.

It's fear that drives B2B marketers to cling to the myth that "serious" buyers only want facts about product features and benefits. Yes, your product saves 23 percent on operational costs and is the first laser laundry in the industry. But does it make your client feel good? Yes, your software integrates seamlessly. But does it make your client's team lives easier? Better? The most powerful B2B campaigns don't sell features; they sell pride, ease, peace of mind, relief, ambition. Efficiency, growth, and so on are important, but they can be implied and amplified creatively. So enough with the soul-crushing whitepapers and lifeless LinkedIn ads. The next time you're tempted to say "disruptive paradigm shift," ask yourself, "Would I say this to a human at a bar?"

Replace "Business" with "People" and suddenly it's "People-to-People." And people love stories. People crave connection. People buy from brands that make them feel like heroes, not spreadsheets.

So go ahead, inject some drama into your next case study. Turn your CEO or sales leaders into a podcast of storytellers and build community around them. Make your webinar less "industry insights" and more "Ted Talk meets *Succession*." Because in the end, even the most stoic executive is still a person. And nobody ever changed the world by participating in a webinar titled "Leveraging End-to-End Solutions."

8 The Digital Marketing Ecosystem: A Strategic Framework for the Algorithmic Age

We are living in an era defined by asymmetric attention economies, where short-termism is a force propelling platforms like Meta to obscene profits and stratospheric valuations. This hyper-optimized landscape, while lucrative for these companies and their investors, has birthed a paradox: the illusion of precision (likes, click-through rates, viral metrics) obscures the erosion of strategic depth. Digital marketing's democratization, powered by AdTech's algorithmic alchemy, has reshaped access but not necessarily wisdom. Add to that a generation of enterprises addicted to dashboards but starved of discernment.

To navigate this terrain, we must reframe creativity beyond aesthetics. True ingenuity lies in structural innovation in reframing and reimagining how people actually bridge their online and offline lives. In this chapter, we dissect the digital marketing taxonomy through a lens of strategic foresight and systemic critique.

1. Search Dynamics: The Battle for Search Is a War on Your Budget

For now, let's talk about what we think we know for sure (you read that right: I refer you to humility because you never know when you hand the reigns to Google). Organic search (SEO)—the industry lie is this is a free way to generate traffic to your website. Under no uncertain terms, that is untrue, and I chose those words freely and carefully. Far from "free traffic," SEO is a high-stakes arms race against the machine learning models that reward semantic depth, EEAT (experience, expertise, authoritativeness, trustworthiness), and latent semantic indexing. The myth of "set-and-forget" SEO stubbornly persists across the business spectrum, yet modern search demands continuous content evolution, entity optimization, and backlink ecosystems that mimic organic human curiosity, not robotic keyword stuffing. While SEO applies to all search engines, I am referring to Google here because it owns 85 percent of search.

We consider relying on SEO a business risk we are not willing to take. Marketing tourists love SEO. Everyone wants to talk SEO, but many simply don't understand the dynamics involved. Our position is SEO should play a role in any marketing strategy, but in the grand scheme of things, it's not that important. I would even go as far as to say it's a waste of time and resources, and here's why.

SEO is a gamble because it requires businesses to react to its whims. Google updates its algorithms abruptly, which means your investment in today's SEO effort and what was working for your site yesterday may not work today. SEO is insatiable. It requires you to keep feeding it, until the next algo change. So, you're inevitably stuck in this circle of SEO hell. No, thank you.

We prefer to have full control over bringing relevant traffic to our clients' websites. Rather than fully invest in SEO, we choose search engine marketing (SEM). SEM in this context is paid Google advertising, although you can buy ads on Bing, Yahoo, and others. The nuance here is to do some SEO and know when it's enough to manage costs and resources, while being more consistent with SEM. By the way, these aren't hard rules. For example, if there's a new dental practice going into an area saturated by dentists who have been there for years and their websites have been up for the same amount of time, there's an uphill, if not a vertical, climb for the new dentist to compete on SEO. On the other hand, the new practice can immediately compete on SEM.

> **"SEO is like chasing ghosts. You spend all this time trying to game Google's algorithm, and then it changes, and you're back to zero. Build a brand people love instead."**
>
> –Mark Cuban, interview on *The Bill Simmons Podcast* (2019).

Google Ads isn't without its own serious black box and bot issues, but SEM at least allows us to control our spend and investment efforts. We can target our audience more precisely by demographics, location, interests, lookalike audiences, possibly intent, and keywords. As much as possible, our goal is to place the ads directly with publishers rather than using Google's programmatic platform, though many times we find the programmatic approach useful. The point is, we pay attention to this part of the game, and so should you. We find SEM, time and again, more cost effective and efficient than SEO. We can also use SEM in brand awareness situations just as we would in print or TV, but the beautiful thing about SEM campaigns is that they can be modified anytime. Notice ad performance issues? No problem, let's dive and change the ad or run A/B tests. Want to add another product? Easy.

2. Social Ecosystems: Attention Arbitrage and Ethical Quagmires

Organic Social

Once a bastion of community-building, as I showed earlier, organic reach now languishes poorly on Meta platforms, and I consider it a tax levied to push brands into paid partnerships. Micro-communities on Discord or Reddit can be an alternative, where niche audiences congregate beyond algorithmic surveillance.[43] But again, building those audiences takes strategy, time, and effort.

Paid Social

Zuckerberg's empire purportedly offers surgical targeting, yet brands increasingly grapple with algorithmic myopia. Case in point: Nike's Instagram carousel ads thrive on visual storytelling, but over-reliance on lookalike audiences risks echo chambers. There's a meme that showed King Charles and Ozzy Ozborn. They're both born in the same year, divorced and remarried, and live in a castle, but chances are they have different interests and buying habits. The cautionary tale is lookalike audiences can be deceiving and downright dangerous. For marketers and policy makers alike, the Cambridge Analytica scandal remains a cautionary tale: data misuse isn't a bug but a feature of surveillance capitalism. The Cambridge Analytica scandal (2018) erupted when it was revealed that the political consulting firm illicitly harvested personal data from up to 87 million Facebook users via a third-party app, which exploited Facebook's lax data-sharing policies to collect information from users and their friends without consent. This data was used to build psychographic profiles to micro-target voters with divisive political ads during the 2016 U.S. election and Brexit campaigns, sparking global outcry over privacy violations and manipulation of democratic processes. Facebook faced massive fines, regulatory scrutiny, and reputational damage, while Cambridge Analytica shut down amid investigations, prompting stricter data laws like the General Data Protection Regulation and reshaping debates on tech ethics and digital privacy.

3. Email and CRM: The Last Bastion of Owned Media

Far from obsolete, experience tells me that email converts more than three times better than social. Tools like Klaviyo now integrate zero-party data (preferences shared voluntarily) to craft narratives that feel less like blasts and more like dialogues. Email offers greater privacy and user control compared to social media, with studies showing it is less susceptible to algorithmic manipulation and data exploitation. Marketers have full control over the database and message. A 2023 Pew Research study found that 72 percent of adults trust email for sensitive communication, versus only 34 percent who trust social media platforms, citing concerns over unauthorized data harvesting (Pew Research Center, 2023). Email providers like Gmail, MailChimp, Constant Contact, and Outlook adhere to stricter regulations (e.g., GDPR, CAN-SPAM) and employ end-to-end encryption tools, whereas social media platforms like Facebook and Instagram have faced fines for privacy violations, including the Cambridge Analytica scandal. Additionally, email boasts higher engagement rates (average open rate of 36.5 percent for marketing emails vs. 1-2 percent organic reach on social media, per Mailchimp, 2023), as users curate their inboxes without algorithmic interference.

4. The Offline-Digital Nexus: Blurring Boundaries

Despite the digital revolution, legacy media like TV and direct mail still perform well due to their reach, tangible engagement, and trusted credibility. Television continues to dominate mass audiences, with Nielsen reporting that 64 percent of U.S. adults watch live TV weekly, and major events like the Super Bowl still draw over 100 million viewers (2023), offering advertisers unmatched scale. Direct mail, often dismissed as outdated, boasts a 90 percent open rate (USPS, 2022) and a 5.3 percent response rate for house lists—23 *times higher* than email's average (MarketingSherpa, 2023). These channels thrive where digital saturation falters: TV leverages sight, sound, and motion to build emotional brand recall, while direct mail's tactile nature cuts through digital clutter, with 60 percent of consumers saying physical ads feel more personal (CRAFTCMS, 2023). Trust also plays a role—73 percent of consumers find TV ads credible (Kantar, 2022), and direct mail avoids algorithm-driven privacy concerns plaguing social platforms.

Skepticism should be directed at every medium and channel, including TV. Any platform selected, whether TV, billboards, radio, magazines, and so on, should necessarily reflect the behavior or your audience. This may sound too simplistic to any marketing pro, but you'd be surprised how much organizational dynamics and politics plays in media selection. As I've demonstrated earlier, there are areas of business where power trumps data and common sense, and I am sure many readers have experienced that.

Okay, let's get back to television! Like the internet, it's still ubiquitous and plays an important part in our lives. Since the advent of the internet, people have been calling for the demise of television. Cord cutting is real and cable numbers are down dramatically. There's no question the mass influence of TV is waning. Since 2010, the pay TV penetration rate in the U.S. has dropped from 88 to 71 percent,[44] and according to Statista, one in three Americans were likely to cancel their cable TV subscription in 2022.[45] Okay, great. So what? Cord cutters still watch networks like ESPN, HBO, and Discovery, so who cares if they stream their TV or get cable? From around Thanksgiving to year-end, American women are glued to the Hallmark Channel for its Christmas movies. From September to March, NFL and NCAA Basketball fans are glued to TV networks like CBS, ESPN, the Big Ten Network, and FS1. Those interested in financial markets religiously tune into CNBC, while politics are the realm of CNN, MSNBC, and FOX.

Yet, television has evolved through streaming and apps. Some would argue that the rise of Netflix, Hulu, HBO Max, and YouTube puts the medium solidly in the media mix consideration for media buyers. According to Mordor Intelligence, the U.S. smart TV market is seeing significant growth, with an increasing adoption of OLED and Quantum Dot (QLED) technology. OLED TV revenue rose 11 percent to $3.3 billion in 2022.[46] Loyalty to networks and the set itself are long gone, but loyalty to content isn't. It's about programming and the audiences it attracts. For example, there are pockets of strong growth in American sports. In 2023, sports programming like the NFL delivered massive audiences for the CBC, NBC, and ABC. According to ESPN, "NFL regular-season games averaged 17.9 million viewers in 2023, tied for the second highest since averages were first tracked in 1995. Buoyed by increases of at least 24 percent in two of the five packages, the first year of the league's new television contracts saw a total increase of 7 percent from last season."[47] Variety lists the NFL's line-up as the top three in its "100 Most Watched TV Series."[48] Due to the Caitlin Clark phenomenon, the WNBA experienced record-setting audience growth in 2024, delivering its most-watched regular season in 24 years with over 54 million unique viewers across multiple networks. Viewership on ESPN platforms saw a 170 percent increase, averaging 1.19 million viewers, while CBS Sports reported an 86 percent increase. ION and NBA TV also reported significant viewership growth, with ION up 133 percent. The 2024 WNBA All-Star Game attracted a record 3.4 million viewers, a 305 percent increase from last season.[49]

In 2022, Amazon Prime began to stream Thursday night football, promising to usher in a new era of immersive sports viewing that may include sports betting and merchandising in the near future. One thing is for sure, television offers dizzying programming options, which can be a haven for larger, well-known brands but can pose a significant challenge for middle market and small businesses. For most businesses, broadcast television and national buys are usually out of reach and local cable is cumbersome to buy, despite its latest nod to digital. Technology is promising to give smaller brands access to TV audiences in the same way Google and social media became a place for small business.

Enter OTT (over-the-top) advertising that delivers ads through streaming media services that are directly offered to viewers over the internet, bypassing traditional cable, broadcast, and satellite TV platforms. Innovators like Vibe (I have no dog in this fight) are promising big access to TV audiences for small dollars with similar dashboard and analytics set up as Google. Businesses can find and target audiences for as little as $500 a month. Whether you're a local cosmetic surgeon or a national truck brand, you can tap into audiences much like you can on Google.

Companies like Vibe are game-changers in terms of audience access and agility, providing easier access to TV audiences that were previously out of reach for many businesses. No more buying cable zones, which seem so 1980ish.

The numbers for television seem to be all over the place. One minute they hint at its demise and the following week they sing its triumphs. Regardless, television is one platform among many, and the game is about audiences and programming. What programs do your audience watch? It's as simple as that.

5. The Social Media Mirage: Hype vs. Strategic Utility

I hate to browbeat this subject, but it deserves it. The key is *platform agnosticism*: using social not as a megaphone but as a listening grid to inform broader strategies. Time and again, social media's strategic utility is frequently overshadowed by inflated expectations. As we discussed earlier, while 4.9 billion or so people use social media globally, organic reach for brands is pitiful. True value in social lies in community-building. For

166 Irresponsibly Digital

instance, brands that align social strategies with email and in-person events may see higher conversion rates.

The Path Forward: Ethical Foresight in a Fractured Landscape

Marketers will continue to be bombarded by a typhoon of technologies promising better, faster, easier, and cheaper marketing. In everything we do, we must resist and transcend short-termism because the alternative is expensive, inefficient, and ineffective. As AI copywriters and synthetic influencers enter the fray, the winners will be those who wield technology not as a crutch but as a collaborator, augmenting human creativity, while sometimes automating it.

In this algorithmic age, the brands that thrive will be those that recognize a timeless truth: Marketing isn't about controlling the narrative. It's about curating meaning in a world drowning in noise.

Walk Confidently. Don't Chase.

The obsession with chasing the "right" platform or any platform is misplaced. TikTok today, AI tomorrow is a distraction from the only metric that truly matters: *who's listening*, not where they're gathered. A devoted audience in a dimly lit bookstore, a niche Substack read by 500 fervent subscribers, or a local podcast with die-hard listeners holds more power than a million disengaged followers on a trending app. History's most iconic brands weren't built on medium-specific gimmicks but on cultivating communities that transcended channels: Harley-Davidson riders forging bonds at rallies long before Instagram or Oprah's book club turning paperbacks into cultural events without algorithms. The medium is merely a vessel, a train that we can get on and off at any time, not the destination. What matters is whether your audience leans in, trusts your voice, and returns not because of the platform's bells and whistles, but because you've become indispensable to their lives. A newsletter can spark a revolution, a church bulletin can birth a movement, and a dinner party can ignite a trend. When you focus on building communities consistently rather than chasing *trends*, the channel becomes irrelevant. After all,

Shakespeare or the Jerky Boys didn't need social media. Shakespeare had the Globe Theatre and the Jerky Boys had cassette tapes.

"But what about *authenticity*?" you may be asking. I really hate this word and its use in marketing and business in general. Products either appeal to customers or they don't. It's the job of the brand or business to make themselves appealing enough for the customer to keep buying. It's the job of the brand and business to get customers to feel something about them. Is that authenticity? I don't know. If Whole Foods suddenly drops its prices, will that be considered inauthentic by its loyal customers? Or will their customers say, "Hell yeah!" On the flip side, in the advertising world, ads that "feel" authentic and genuine can connect with the audience on a deeper level. For instance, the Dove Real Beauty campaign challenged conventional beauty standards and celebrated diverse body types and skin tones. Audiences connected with the much talked about message of that campaign, which was momentary. Dove has since moved on; does that mean Dove's brand is inauthentic? No, it means that campaign was meant for a particular moment in time and now is a different time for a different message.

How to Build Campaigns

When crafting a marketing campaign, I anchor every decision to two non-negotiable pillars: intent and emotion. These principles act as the campaign's DNA, shaping every subsequent choice, from audience targeting to distribution channels. Here's why they matter:

1. **Intent: What do I want people to do?** Before designing logos, writing copy, or choosing platforms, I define the *action* I want the audience to take. Is it to buy a product? Sign up for a newsletter? Donate to a cause? This "north star" ensures the campaign isn't just creative, but *purposeful*. For example, if the goal is to drive app downloads, every element, from ad visuals to the call-to-action, must eliminate friction between interest and action. Intent answers the "why" behind the campaign, transforming vague goals ("raise awareness") into measurable outcomes ("increase trial sign-ups by 25 percent in Q3").

2. **Emotion: How do I want people to feel?** Logic makes people think; emotion makes them act. Whether it's nostalgia, urgency, joy, or fear, emotion is the lever that moves audiences from passive observers to active participants. A luxury watch ad might evoke pride and legacy ("This heirloom will outlive you."), while a climate nonprofit's campaign might stir guilt or hope ("Act now, or lose the Arctic."). Emotion is about *resonance*.

Only then comes the "how." Once intent and emotion are crystalized, the tactical questions fall into place:

- **Audience.** Who is most likely to feel this emotion and act on this intent? A B2B cybersecurity firm targeting IT directors might leverage fear of data breaches, while a skincare brand for teens might tap into the desire for social acceptance.

- **Distribution.** Where does this emotion land hardest? A heartfelt documentary-style video might thrive on YouTube, while a snappy, anxiety-driven meme could dominate TikTok.

- **Messaging.** What language, tone, and visuals amplify the desired feeling? A charity combating hunger might use stark, visceral imagery of empty plates, while a meditation app could pair serene visuals with minimalist copy.

While this approach is slower, it avoids the common trap of starting with tactics ("Let's make a viral video!") and forces marketers to ask, "Does this ad/event/post serve the core intent and emotion?" If not, it's noise. For instance, Dollar Shave Club's launch video didn't just sell razors; it channeled frustration with overpriced grooming products (emotion) into a clear intent: "Subscribe now and stop wasting money." The result was 12,000 sign-ups in 48 hours. Someone had to understand the economics of the business and tap into customer emotions while conceiving and producing the company's first campaign. Marketing is about engineering a response. By starting with intent and emotion, you're not just chasing clicks or impressions; you're building campaigns that resonate, endure, and are highly accretive to your business.

Integrated Campaigns vs. Tactics

A tactic is a tool. How you use the tool is your strategy, and how tactics are used together over a period of time that focuses on a single message is your campaign. Depending on your business goals, tactics may be all you need. For example, if you're a restaurateur, building a loyal following on Instagram to showcase your menu items may be all you need right now. It may also be all you can do well realistically because of budget or resource limitations. If you're a national engineering company in the B2B space with plenty of resources, it may make sense to use LinkedIn to build your network and showcase your work in between tradeshows.

Why Obsessing Over Competitors Is a Deadly Distraction

Paying attention to competitors is prudent, but mistaking their playbook for gospel is a dangerous recipe for mediocrity and sometimes outright failure. Competitors may be chasing trends, misreading their audience, or clinging to outdated tactics. After all, how can we know if their strategies are rooted in insight or inertia, in internal power and politics? For every Apple that reshapes an industry, there are a hundred brands blindly copying each other into a sea of sameness.

True differentiation doesn't come from mirroring rivals; it comes from understanding your unique value so deeply that competitors become irrelevant. Red Bull didn't overtake Coca-Cola by mimicking soda ads; it literally created an alternate universe of extreme sports and cultural events that redefined energy drinks as a lifestyle by bringing people together. Focus on your audience's unmet needs, your brand's irreplaceable strengths, and the stories only you can tell. Competitors are a weathervane, not a compass. The moment you fixate on their moves, you surrender your power to chart your own course.

Integrated Marketing: The Unstoppable Force That Silences the Noise

What we want to avoid is reactionary marketing or dropping marketing bombs. That's expensive and downright amateur hour. Integrated marketing is a philosophy that takes a global approach to marketing communication by using a variety of channels and tactics either at the same time or along the same time continuum. It allows for consistency of message across all channels and platforms by deploying campaigns to multiple channels to target its intended audience. When agility is inserted into integrated strategy, it becomes a potent tool, an advantage in my experience.

By fusing channels into a seamless, global narrative, you reach deeper and more efficiently. Why settle for a whisper when you can orchestrate a crescendo? Of course, budget is key, but while competitors cling to single-channel tactics, integrated campaigns transform risk into ruthlessness. A failed Facebook ad can be irrelevant when your other channels, like email, podcast appearances, and four annual events pick up the slack.

Think of it as teaching a masterclass in persuasion in several different classrooms. Just as great teachers tailor lessons to visual learners, hands-on tinkerers, and analytical minds, integrated marketing infiltrates every corner of your audience's universe. The social scroller, the LinkedIn lurker, the podcast commuter—none escape the gravitational pull of your message. Again, budget and resources will drive your decisions about placement. This isn't about "covering bases." It's about *owning the field* to the extent your resources allow.

Imagine offline and digital platforms working together to drive your message. At the center of any integrated campaign is your creative messaging. That message must be molded to be implemented or fit on the appropriate platform or channel. It's important to recognize the distinction between integrated marketing and omni-channel advertising. Integrated marketing is not omni-channel advertising. Omni-channel advertising is a subcategory of integrated marketing. For instance, integrated marketing can include public relations, events, key opinion leader engagement, tradeshow display, sales, and omni-channel advertising. Omni-channel advertising can include television, radio, and outdoor advertising. At the core of marketing strategy is the product, price, distribution, and customer service. All this stuff goes into the hopper to make marketing successes, mediocrity, or failure.

Think of integrated marketing as if you were a top mutual fund manager. Your job is to identify assets that will deliver the best return possible and allocate a portion of your budget to each asset appropriately. Under-investment may lead to poor performance and over-investment can lead to waste, begging the question, what is the optimal balance? "It depends" is not the answer you're looking for, but it's the correct answer. Anyone who gives you a definitive answer to this should also be prepared to give you next week's winning lottery numbers.

Resources: Budget and Talent

Here's the understatement of the millennia: budget is very important if you want to get marketing stuff done. A $10 million campaign will look and feel different than a $5 million or $1 million campaign, which will look and feel different than a $150,000 campaign and different than a $15,000 campaign. But sometimes, the $15,000 campaign can have an out-sized impact because of the talent running it.

As we discussed early in this book, on the basketball court, Michael Jordan and I have one thing in common. He was a guard and so was I. Do you want Michael Jordan or Abe Kasbo taking the winning shot at the end of a basketball game? The answer is insanely simple. It works the same way with marketing talent. Just because you have a position of "Director of Marketing" or you hire a "creative agency" doesn't mean you're engaging talent.

Hiring talent, without question, is akin to putting together a sports team. You have the power to draft Michael Jordan or someone else. It may be a cliché to say, but your business and maybe career depend on your team. While building a basketball team, it's necessary to bring in players and coaches experienced in the sport; in marketing, specific experience in the field is nice, but not necessary. The people at Coke aren't asking "Hey, what do you know about selling sugar water?" The people at AmEx aren't necessarily asking, "What do you know about selling financial products?" What they are more likely to ask is "What good ideas do you have?" because ideas are the engine of marketing. So, when you're interviewing in-house talent or agencies, rather than asking them what they know about your industry, which they can easily learn quickly, discuss and debate marketing ideas. Be sure to bring your humility and skepticism with you. Everyone is a marketing genius these days and you need to separate bullshitters from real talent. At the same time, just because you're personally uncomfortable with some of those ideas doesn't mean they're bad; it means you're uncomfortable. It's more important than ever to ensure the people you hire, including agencies, aren't bullshitting you.

9 Market Research

Everyone talks about business leadership, but in marketing, some business leaders cling to "market research" or "customer voice" to get a pulse of the market or as a similar tactic of using analytics as a tool to justify XYZ. Of course, there are legit and worthy market research projects. Perhaps I'm in the wrong crowd, because in my experience, especially lately, market research has become a convenient tool rooted in self-preservation. Research is often produced to create a veneer of authority and justification for campaigns. There's an inescapable reality here that we must address. If you're a marketer on the "inside," research is a vital tool to help move projects along and gain credibility with your bosses. If you're an agency, research is a lifeline for your campaign go/no-go decisions or direction. But not all research or opinion gathering are created equal.

Jeff Bezos didn't need a focus group to ask people if they wanted to buy books online, and Steve Jobs didn't ask anyone's opinion about the iPod or iPhone. Now you're saying, "Wait a minute. I'm not Steve Jobs or Jeff Bezos." Consider the case of Sony's co-founder and CEO,

> **"Data and feedback are tools, not answers. If we'd listened to customers who wanted DVDs forever, there'd be no Netflix streaming."**
>
> —Reed Hastings, co-founder, Netflix

Akio Morita. Had he listened to his market research team, which concluded that no one wanted a personal music device, he would have killed the Sony Walkman. But Morita questioned Sony's market research because he saw limitations in its ability to accurately predict consumer behavior. He believed that people didn't always know what they wanted until they saw it or experienced it—cue Amazon, iPhone, Pet Rock, and so on.

From the 1970s to the early '90s, Sony sold over 200 million Walkmans worldwide in the face of substantial market research predicting the failure of the product. It was the idea of personal listening that made the Walkman a must-have, not the product itself. The birth of this idea is rooted in Akio Morita's willingness to take the risk. By believing in his instincts and not relying on market research to guide decision-making, the Walkman became a seminal cultural phenomenon that would go on to inspire countless products. Morita famously said, "The secret of success in business is not to follow but to lead."

Look, I'm not saying asking people's opinion isn't useful. It is. Yes, you can get some information from asking people what they think about your campaigns or products, but as we discussed, this approach is fraught with danger, which can lead to failures and lost opportunities. Creative leadership, for the most part, sits outside mainstream thinking. Creativity itself requires conviction, courage, vision, and some level of risk. I mentioned Bezos and Jobs earlier, but there's also Budweiser's iconic Whassup? Superbowl campaign in 2000. The most memorable campaigns or products are ones that required risk.

Asking people their opinion puts businesses in a tough situation. MBA programs demand students justify their vision with "research." Yet pitfalls are aplenty in asking people what they think. Groupthink is one issue when asking people what they think in a forum or focus groups; the other is consensus. The NFL didn't ask whether people wanted to pay outlandishly more for their seats by purchasing "the right" to buy their seats. They did it, and stadiums are overflowing!

The mere presence of a moderator, business owner, or CEO in a forum can influence the direction of the response. People aren't always honest; they may take into account other people's positions, which contributes to unreliable information. They may want to protect what they really think because they are afraid, for whatever reason, to give an honest opinion. If you're sending an email survey, results can be skewed by the $50 gift card you're offering, or by click-happy people who just want to get through the questions. In many ways, while the internet has made things easier, it has also made them more complex. Everything is seemingly more accessible, giving marketers the illusion that technology can produce "accurate" research. Tools like Survey Monkey or even "Hey, what do you think of this?" in an email can produce "opinions" often without context or detail, which is needed to understand the motivation behind the feedback.

Let's look at New Coke again. Coca-Cola was deep into the Cola wars with Pepsi in the late 1970s and early '80s, which produced both group-think and tunnel vision among its executives. Somehow, in response to Pepsi's product formulation and messaging, Coca-Cola convinced itself, through its own market research, that consumers wanted a sweeter, smoother taste. Imagine achieving success for about 80 years with the same formula that allowed your products to almost replace water on dinner tables around the world and thinking, "We must respond to our competitor's formula by changing our product." So here, Coca-Cola failed to appreciate its own brand's cultural power. It forgot what its own CEO Roberto Goizueta once said in a 1993 interview with *Fortune,* "A Coke is a smile, a handshake, a spark of optimism. We don't market a product; we market the essence of human connection. That's why a Coke in a child's hand in Buenos Aires means the same as one in Berlin." Coke made the mistake of getting more in the weeds in its efforts to take on Pepsi, and in the process, it found itself in a competitive fog in which it failed to understand the essence of why people loved it. It was the emotional connection that consumers had to the original Coca-Cola formula that made it a success. People who loved the original formula were angry, and some formed protest groups! People liked the way Coke tasted, so why change? Because of the Pepsi challenge? Pepsi's messaging or investment in advertising? Coke had plenty of money to combat messaging in the marketplace, but they seemingly went for Pepsi's head fake and, in the case of New Coke, lost the battle, and damaged the brand at the same time. So, in its intent to give people what Coke thought they wanted, Coca-Cola's New Coke adventure was destined for failure from the start.

Business is awash with examples of market research leading them astray. In 2011, J.C. Penney, the sluggish retailer, hired Ron Johnson, a former Apple executive, to reimagine its position in the market and revitalize the business. Based on consumer research, Johnson introduced a new pricing strategy and a shift away from promotions and sales. Despite making specific changes based on asking people what they think, sales and market share continued to decline, which led to Johnson's demise as CEO. J.C. Penny eventually undid many of the changes Johnson had implemented.

On the flipside, there are plenty of examples of market research success, including Netflix's decision to invest in original content production. Netflix's market research indicated a growing demand for high-quality content exclusive to its platform. Exclusive programming helped drive over 200 million subscribers to Netflix, helping maintain its juggernaut status in the space. In 2007, Fitbit was founded on a hunch, which led to extensive market research where it found growing demand for fitness trackers that could help people monitor their daily physical activity. Fitbit's research discovered that many people were interested in tracking their physical activity but found existing products to be cumbersome and unreliable. Based on its research, the company refined its product offering to create a stylish, simple product that was launched with rave reviews in 2009 with millions of units sold since.

Confirmation bias is a silent saboteur of marketing or any research. Confirmation bias tricks us into seeking, interpreting, and favoring information that aligns with our pre-existing beliefs, while dismissing evidence that challenges them. This tendency is dangerously amplified when paired with "sample-of-one" thinking, the habit of overgeneralizing from a single personal experience. "When I go the dentist, I see XYZ." "When I go to the mall, there's this or that." "I've never bought anything from Facebook." We all have our biases and experiences. Let's make sure we understand this tenant because applying biases to solve marketing problems or develop strategies is a terrible idea. We want to stay away from the illusion of significance: Imagine someone tries a new diet, loses five pounds in a week, and declares it a miracle. They then cherry-pick success stories online, ignoring studies showing the diet's long-term risks. Their initial experience (a random fluctuation, not proof) becomes a "seminal event," warping their judgment.

The echo chamber effect is also a dangerous place. When we ask others for input but only heed opinions that mirror our own, we create a feedback loop of delusion. For instance, a consumer electronics startup, fueled by initial success with young, urban early adopters through targeted social media ads and influencer partnerships, becomes trapped in a marketing echo chamber. The team, primarily composed of individuals from similar demographics who actively consume the same platforms, relentlessly refines campaigns based solely on engagement metrics and feedback loops from this existing, narrow audience segment. They dismiss exploratory market research into older demographics or suburban families, overlook potential in underutilized channels like email marketing or strategic retail partnerships, and interpret any plateauing growth solely as a need for more social media spend or trendier influencers, rather than a signal to diversify their approach. Consequently, they fail to expand their market reach, become overly vulnerable to algorithm changes on their primary platforms, and miss significant growth opportunities beyond their initial bubble, ultimately leading to stagnation as they keep shouting the same message to an audience that's either saturated or not the only one that matters.

This is not easy to do but, when possible, actively seek disconfirming evidence. If you believe your marketing campaign is flawless, ask, "What would prove me wrong?" Challenge your assumptions like a scientist, not a lawyer defending a case. Truth thrives when we stop needing to be right.

I mentioned earlier in this book that I don't particularly care about personal views when I work with clients. And that's not easy, but it's necessary. Marketers set aside personal opinions and experiences because they add no meaningful insights or value aside from personal experience. We have to get outside of ourselves to draw more precise conclusions about our business and marketing approach. Our work with clients is to challenge their personal assumptions and biases, which can lead to uncomfortable conversations. Our job is to be honest with our clients, and that may include hurting their feelings a bit. (We do it nicely, because no one's baby is ugly, of course.) But it is better to temporarily hurt feeling than lose opportunity or market share.

10 Reviving the Soul of Marketing: A Future Beyond Data Worship

The bad news is we're living in the dizzying age of the Clickocracy. I am sure they'll continue to consolidate their power through alliances of platform evangelists, growth hackers, and analytics peddlers who, up to today, have successfully convinced businesses that salvation lies solely in the digital realm. The good news is people are waking up in many of the vast quarters throughout the industry. Recently, Bose paused its paid search ads in half its US markets. In a June 19, 2025 interview with *Adweek*, CMO Jim Mollica suggest that Google was taking more credit for driving sales than it deserved. "In the industry, the question has always been how incremental is paid Google Search, specifically around brand terms?"[50] To be clear, businesses that continue to irresponsibly allocate most of their marketing efforts into the digital basket usually end up benefiting tech bros, not themselves. Let's break down this costly delusion and move to a wiser path.

1. The Great Digital Mirage: Big Tech Wins; Businesses Often Lose

Just as a Judas goat leads other animals to a specific destination, including slaughter, Clickocrats are relentless in their singular focus to profit from pushing the digital drug. Businesses, fearing irrelevance or being left behind, dutifully comply, pouring budgets into platform ads and chasing algorithmic favor. Clickocrats ask us to trust analytics dashboards flashing superficial numbers: likes, shares, follower counts, conversions, cart abandonment, and so on. But what do they really mean? A million views from irrelevant audiences or bot farms? A thousand likes (by whom?) that never translate to a single sale? These metrics create an illusion of success or failure while obscuring true business impact: profit, loyal customers, brand equity. Tech platforms are happy to sell you ads and demand content generation from your business in return for vanity metrics. Be diligent; question the principles of your digital strategies. Again, of course you should be engaging in the digital sphere, but the question is *how*.

The real winners are found in the quarterly reports of Meta, Google, and TikTok. Their astronomical advertising revenues are built on businesses' fear of missing out and their unquestioning faith in often-opaque analytics. It's a lopsided ecosystem: businesses pay increasing ad costs and get decreasing organic reach on platforms they don't control, while Big Tech companies rake in profits.

Remember the "pivot to video" craze that went on for a few years between 2015 and 2017? Clickocrats and platforms like Facebook heavily pushed video as the future. Major publishers and media outlets alike laid off writers en masse to invest heavily in Facebook video content. Result? Facebook later admitted to inflating video view metrics, and algorithm changes drastically reduced organic reach. Many publishers who bet the farm were decimated, while Facebook's ad revenue soared. The tech giant won; businesses lost.

2. Strategic Selection: Slow and Steady Beats Reactionary Panic

The antidote to Clickocracy and beating them at their own game isn't abandoning digital; it's intentional and often restrained deployment of digital tools along with their offline counterparts. There's no two ways about it: businesses must stop being reactionary (jumping on every trend, fearing every algorithm update) and start being thoughtful architects of their marketing approach, including their digital presence.

In your digital marketing, choose platforms and tactics that actually fit your business. Does your hospital or distribution company really need a viral TikTok dance? Probably not. A bespoke furniture maker might find far more value in detailed Pinterest inspiration or Instagram videos showcasing craftsmanship than Twitter postings. Choose platforms where your ideal customer genuinely spends time and engages meaningfully.

Similarly, consider which type of reach would work best for your business. Is "reach" about shouting at as many people as possible? Or whispering meaningfully to the right people? Quality over quantity. A newsletter reaching 5,000 highly engaged potential clients is infinitely more valuable than a post seen (and ignored) by 500,000 irrelevant scrollers. A lunch meeting with ten prospects is infinitely more valuable than buying Facebook ads. Stillness is better than reactive noise.

In its early days, Glossier exploded by leveraging Instagram and its own blog (Into the Gloss) to build a passionate community around user-generated content and authentic beauty conversations. They focused intensely on platforms where their beauty-obsessed audience lived and engaged deeply, rather than trying to be everywhere at once.

3. The Timeless Core: Human Connection Is King (Digital or Not)

Strip away the algorithms and the hype, and marketing remains fundamentally human. It's about forging connections, evoking emotions, and solving problems through creativity and storytelling. Whether you're on Instagram, at a trade show, or sending a direct mailer, this lasting principle holds.

Remember that emotion drives action. People buy based on how they feel. Does your marketing presence spark joy, inspire trust, alleviate a fear, or foster belonging? Recall Dove's Real Beauty campaign: it was rooted in a deep emotional truth about self-esteem, not just clicks.

In a sea of generic ads, lookalike campaigns, and trend-chasing, genuine creativity stands out. Apple's iconic campaign, Shot on iPhone, focused on stunning visuals and human experience, showcasing product benefits through emotion and artistry, not just specs and sales pitches. By the way, that campaign was made for TV as well as social.

One more thing to consider: no digital anything. What are you doing with your non-digital strategies? And how are you doing it?

A Glimpse Into the Future

As we stand at the crossroads of marketing's journey, I'd like to envision a future that marries the power of meaningful data with the richness of human experience. This future is one where marketers harness the insights provided by analytics but use them as stepping stones, not crutches. It's a future where brands tell stories that touch hearts, create experiences that inspire, and build connections that endure.

The digital marketing era began with a seductive promise: democratization. Tools once reserved for Fortune 500 budgets, such as global reach, hyper-targeting, and real-time analytics, were suddenly accessible to startups, middle market companies, and solopreneurs. But like all revolutions, this one came with hidden costs. We traded intuition for dashboards, storytelling for clickbait, and expertise for algorithmic obedience. In our frenzy to embrace these tools, businesses have made a fatal miscalculation by conflating everything digital with marketing. Today, marketers navigate a landscape where viral is conflated with valuable, where likes masquerade as loyalty, and where the pressure to perform (not persuade) has turned entire industries into digital sharecroppers, toiling on platforms that profit from their labor.

This book is a reminder that impactful marketing transcends screens. It's the primal thrill of a Coca-Cola "Hilltop" ad uniting the world in song, the visceral punch of Apple's "1984" spot rebelling against conformity, the quiet authority of a New Yorker print ad that whispers, "This is for the intellectually elite." Digital tactics are merely channels, not the essence. Yet we've allowed platforms, clicks, likes, and algorithm hacks to overshadow timeless principles: understanding human desire, building indelible brand mythos, and forging emotional bonds that outlast any platform's lifespan. This book has argued that marketing's greatest crisis isn't technological; it's existential. We've outsourced our craft to machines and tech giants, surrendered our judgment to A/B tests, and forgotten that the most powerful campaigns, from Nike's Just Do It to Dove's Real Beauty succeeded not because they optimized for CTRs, but because they reframed how we see ourselves. To survive the algorithmic age, marketers must rediscover their humanity, and fast.

The Final Word: Marketing as a Force for Good

The word "irresponsibly" in this book's title isn't an insult; it's a diagnosis. Marketers must reclaim their role as storytellers, psychologists, and cultural architects. Right now, marketers are being forced to be data merchants, scrubbing spreadsheets for scraps of insight. But it's not too late. It's not too late to create the next cultural moment for your business, whether you are the CMO of a publicly traded company, a startup, or the owner of a Main Street shop.

Imagine a future where marketers are again respected as stewards of trust, where campaigns are measured not by clicks but by cultural impact. This future isn't built on AI or blockchain. It's built on courage, the courage to unplug from the hype machine, to reject "best practices," and to create work that matters.

As you close this book, ask yourself: will you be remembered as a caretaker of brands, or a cog in the algorithmic machine? The answer lies not in your tech stack, but in your willingness to embrace marketing's oldest truth: people don't buy products; they buy better versions of themselves.

The path forward isn't easy, but it's the only one that leads somewhere. Now go make something worth buying. And always dribble with your head up.

Notes

1 Thompson, Ben, "An Interview With Meta CEO Mark
   Zuckerberg About AI and the Evolution of Social Media,"
   Stratechery, May 1, 2025, *https://stratechery.com/2025/
   an-interview-with-meta-ceo-mark-zuckerberg-about-ai-
   and-the-evolution-of-social-media/*.

2 Karlovitch, Sara, "Marketing Campaign Issues Multiply:
   Here's What the Numbers Say," Marketing Dive, February
   28, 2025, *www.marketingdive.com/news/marketing-
   campaign-issues-multiply-heres-what-numbers/741014/*.

3 Feger, Arielle, "Digital Media Makes up Nearly Two-
   thirds of Consumers' Total Time Spent With Media,"
   eMarketer, August 13, 2024, *www.emarketer.com/content/
   digital-media-makes-up-nearly-two-thirds-of-consumers-
   total-time-spent-with-media*.

4 Pelchen, Lexie, "Internet Usage Statistics in 2025," *Forbes*,
   March 1, 2024, *www.forbes.com/home-improvement/
   internet/internet-statistics/*.

5   Barthel, Michael, "Newspapers Fact Sheet," Pew Research Center, April 24, 2025, *www.pewresearch.org/journalism/fact-sheet/newspapers/*.

6   "Number of Pay TV Households in the U.S. 2019-2028," Statista, July 4, 2024, *www.statista.com/statistics/251268/number-of-pay-tv-households-in-the-us/*.

7   Benen, Steve, "Friday Nightcap: The Future of Elon Musk's Influence," MSNBC, August 7, 2024, *www.msnbc.com/rachel-maddow-show/maddowblog/new-suit-musks-x-accuses-advertisers-boycotting-platform-twitter-takeo-rcna165550*.

8   Fou, Augustine, "My Q&A About Ad Fraud With a Skeptical CMO," *Forbes*, January 21, 2021, *www.forbes.com/sites/augustinefou/2021/01/21/my-qa-about-ad-fraud-with-a-skeptical-cmo/*.

9   Lumer, Riane, "Conserving your superpower, which is your attention span," CNN, August 11, 2024, *www.cnn.com/2024/08/11/health/how-to-increase-attention-span-wellness*.

10 McClellan, Steve, "MAD: ANA Finds as Much as $20B Wasted on Programmatic Ad Buys," MediaPost, June 19, 2023, *www.mediapost.com/publications/article/386433/ana-finds-13-20-billion-may-be-wasted-in-open-we.html*.

11 Haggin, Patience, "Google Violated Its Standards in Ad Deals, Research Finds," *The Wall Street Journal*, June 27, 2023, *www.wsj.com/tech/google-violated-its-standards-in-ad-deals-research-finds-3e24e041*.

12 Morgan, Dave, "YouTube Debacle Tip of the Industry Iceberg," MediaPost, June 29, 2023, *www.mediapost.com/publications/article/386835/youtube-debacle-tip-of-the-industry-iceberg.html*.

13 "Did Google Mislead Advertisers About TrueView Skippable In-stream Ads for the Past Three Years?" Adalytics, n.d., *https://adalytics.io/blog/invalid-google-video-partner-trueview-ads*.

14 Dunkley, Emma, Jim Pickard, and Cristina Criddle, "Meta Singled Out by UK Financial Lobby Group Over Digital Scams," *Financial Times*, July 8, 2023, *www.ft.com/content/d0215c7c-90e5-4e53-b5ea-a19140730b21*.

15 Horwitz, Jeff and Angel Au-Yeung, "Meta Battles an 'Epidemic of Scams' as Criminals Flood Instagram and Facebook," *The Wall Street Journal*, May 15, 2025, *www.wsj.com/tech/meta-fraud-facebook-instagram-813363c8*.

16 Richabadas, Tushar, "Threat Spotlight: How Bad Bot Traffic Is Changing," Barracuda Blog, October 18, 2023, *https://blog.barracuda.com/2023/10/18/ threat-spotlight-bad-bot-traffic-changing.*

17 Kiernan, John S., "Google Quality Issues: Part of an Intentional Strategy?" WalletHub, February 19, 2025, *https://wallethub.com/blog/ google-quality-issues-report/147091.*

18 "Fake Accounts," Meta, n.d., *https://transparency.meta.com/ reports/community-standards-enforcement/fake-accounts/ facebook/#content-actioned.*

19 Johnson, Lauren, "When Procter & Gamble Cut $200 Million in Digital Ad Spend, It Increased Its Reach 10%," *Adweek*, March 1, 2018, *www.adweek. com/brand-marketing/when-procter-gamble-cut-200-million-in-digital-ad-spend-its-marketing-became-10-more-effective/.*

20 Saad, Lydia, "Military Brass, Judges Among Professions at New Image Lows," Gallup, March 26, 2025, *https://news.gallup.com/poll/388649/military-brass-judges-among-professions-new-image-lows.aspx.*

21 Briggs, Saga,"Six Ways Digital Media Impacts the Brain," NMSBA, n.d., *https://nmsba.com/news/740-six-ways-digital-media-impacts-the-brain.*

22 Dartmouth College, "Digital Media May Be Changing How You Think," ScienceDaily, May 16, 2016, *www.sciencedaily.com/ releases/2016/05/160508151944.htm.*

23 Haynes, Trevor, "Dopamine, Smartphones & You: A Battle for Your Time," SITNBoston, May 1, 2018, *https://unplugged.sunygeneseoenglish.org/ wp-content/uploads/sites/31/2019/11/Domamine-PDF.pdf.*

24 Small, Gary W., Jooyeon Lee, Aaron Kaufman, Jason Jalil, Prabha Siddarth, Himaja Gaddipati, Teena D. Moody, and Susan Y. Bookheimer, "Brain Health Consequences of Digital Technology Use," *Dialogues in Clinical Neuroscience* 22 (2): 179–87, *https://doi.org/10.31887/dcns.2020.22.2/gsmall.*

25 "Technology's Effects on Our Brains & Bodies," Pepperdine University—Boone Center for the Family, August 12, 2020, *https://boonecenter. pepperdine.edu/relationship-iq/blog/posts/technology_effects_on_our_brains_ and_bodies.htm.*

26 Small, Gary W., "Brain Health Consequences of Digital Technology Use."

27 Auletta, Ken, "Excerpt: 'Googled,'" NPR, November 19, 2009, *www.npr.org/2009/11/19/120389927/excerpt-googled.*

28 Enberg, Jasmine, "5 Things to Know About the Creator Economy in 2023," eMarketer, February 23, 2023, *www.emarketer.com/content/5-things-know-about-creator-economy-2023.*

29 Adriel Content Team, "Uber's Useless Digital Ad Campaigns: Detecting Ad Fraud With Centralized Data," Adriel, January 16, 2024, *www.adriel.com/blog/detecting-ad-fraud-with-centralized-data.*

30 Goodwin, Danny, "Huge Google Search document leak reveals inner workings of ranking algorithm," Search Engine Land, May 28, 2024, *https://searchengineland.com/google-search-document-leak-ranking-442617.*

31 "2023 Social Media Industry Benchmark Report," RivalIQ, n.d., *https://get.rivaliq.com/hubfs/eBooks/2023-social-media-benchmark-report.pdf.*

32 Johnson, Lauren, "When Procter & Gamble Cut $200 Million in Digital Ad Spend, It Increased Its Reach 10%."

33 Lee, Jennifer, "Big Tobacco's Spin on Women's Liberation," *The New York Times*, July 7, 2017, *https://archive.nytimes.com/cityroom.blogs.nytimes.com/2008/10/10/big-tobaccos-spin-on-womens-liberation.*

34 Mather, Mark, and Paola Scommegna, "Fact Sheet: Aging in the United States," PRB, January 9, 2024, *www.prb.org/resources/fact-sheet-aging-in-the-united-states/.*

35 "The CMO Survey 2021," Deloitte, January 9, 2022, *www.deloitte.com/il/en/services/consulting/research/the-cmo-survey-2021.html.*

36 "CMO Tenure Study: An Expanded View of CMO Tenure and Backgrounds," SpencerStuart, May 2023, *www.spencerstuart.com/research-and-insight/cmo-tenure-study-an-expanded-view-of-cmo-tenure-and-backgrounds.*

37 Monllos, Kristina, Michael Bürgi, and Seb Joseph, "Transparency shift: CMOs navigate new norms in agency profit models," Digiday, May 17, 2024, *https://digiday.com/media/transparency-shift-cmos-navigate-new-norms-in-agency-profit-models/.*

38 Wager, Emma, Imani Telesford, Shameek Rakshit, Nisha Kurani, and Cynthia Cox, "How does the quality of the U.S. health system compare to other countries?" Health System Tracker, October 9, 2024, *www.healthsystemtracker.org/chart-collection/ quality-u-s-healthcare-system-compare-countries/*.

39 Gunja, Munira Z., Evan D. Gumas, Relebohile Masitha, and Laurie C. Zephyrin, "Insights into the U.S. Maternal Mortality Crisis: An International Comparison," The Commonwealth Fund, June 4, 2024, *www.commonwealthfund.org/publications/issue-briefs/2024/jun/ insights-us-maternal-mortality-crisis-international-comparison*.

40 Reinartz, Werner J. and Peter Saffert, "Creativity in Advertising: When It Works and When It Doesn't," *Harvard Business Review*, June 2013, *https:// hbr.org/2013/06/creativity-in-advertising-when-it-works-and-when-it-doesnt*.

41 Lee, Kristen, "'Death by Pokémon Go': Study finds that driving while playing likely cost billions in car damage, injuries," *Business Insider*, January 11, 2021, *www.businessinsider.com/ pokmon-go-study-driving-playing-cost-millions-car-damage-injuries-2021-1*.

42 Burt, Tequia, "Building a Memorable B2B Brand: Who Will Be the Next Iconic Brand?" LinkedIn, July 1, 2024, *www.linkedin.com/business/ marketing/blog/marketing-collective/building-a-memorable-b2b-brand*.

43 "The 4 Types of Influencers and How to Work With Them," Markerly, December 21, 2021, *https://markerly.com/pulse/types-of-influencers/*.

44 Stoll, Julia, "Pay TV Penetration in the U.S. 2005-2023," Statista, December 3, 2024, *www.statista.com/statistics/467842/pay-tv-penetration-rate-usa/*.

45 Stoll, Julia, "Likelihood to Cut the Cord in the U.S. 2020-2022," Statista, March 20, 2023, *www.statista.com/statistics/325635/ likelihood-cut-the-cord-usa/*.

46 "US Smart TV Market Size & Share Analysis—Growth Trends & Forecasts (2025–2030)," Mordor Intelligence, n.d., *www.mordorintelligence.com/ industry-reports/united-states-smart-tv-market.*.

47 "NFL averages 17.9M viewers in 2023, up 7% from previous year," ESPN, January 10, 2024, *www.espn.com/nfl/story/_/id/39277615/ nfl-averages-179m-viewers-2023-7-previous-year*.

48 Schneider, Michael, "The 100 Most-Watched Telecasts of 2023: NFL, Oscars, Gordon Ramsay, 'NCIS' and a Single 'Yellowstone' Episode," *Variety*, December 29, 2023, *https://variety.com/2023/tv/news/most-watched-shows-2023-ncis-oscars-blue-bloods-super-bowl-yellowstone-1235854795/.*

49 "WNBA Delivers Record-Setting 2024 Season," WNBA, September 27, 2024, *www.wnba.com/news/wnba-delivers-record-setting-2024-season.*

50 Joe, Ryan, "Bose Has Paused Paid Search In Half its US Markets," *Adweek*, June 19, 2025, *www.adweek.com/brand-marketing/bose-has-paused-paid-search-in-the-us*

About the Author

As founder and CEO of Verasoni, Abe Kasbo advises C-Suite executives, business owners, and brands on critical communications, branding, digital transformation, and public relations strategy. His leadership extends beyond the corporate sphere, serving on various boards, as a social entrepreneur and leading humanitarian initiatives.

Abe's unique blend of insights, leadership, and perspective on business and entrepreneurship from a lens of marketing communications have fueled the growth and transformation of Verasoni's clients since its founding in 2005. Kasbo holds a Master's in Public Administration and a Bachelor of Arts in Political Science from Seton Hall University.

www.ingramcontent.com/pod-product-compliance
Lightning Source LLC
Chambersburg PA
CBHW040923210326
41597CB00030B/5161